COSTUMES AND SETTINGS FOR STAGING HISTORICAL PLAYS

Volume I
The Classical Period

COSTUMES AND SETTINGS FOR STAGING HISTORICAL PLAYS

JACK CASSIN-SCOTT

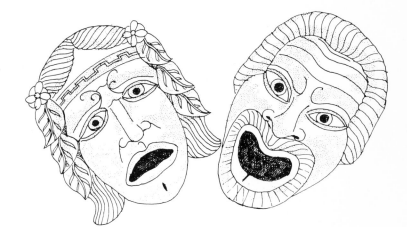

Volume I
The Classical Period

Plays, Inc. *Boston*

© 1979 by Jack Cassin-Scott

First American edition published by Plays, Inc. 1979

Library of Congress Cataloging in Publication Data

Cassin-Scott, Jack.
  Costumes and settings for staging historical plays.

  CONTENTS: v. 1. The classical period. — v. 2. Medieval.

  1. Costume—History. 2. Theaters—Stage-setting and
scenery. 3. Historical drama. I. Title.
PN2067.C33 1979   792'.025   78-26037
ISBN 0-8238-0231-0 (v. 1)

Printed in Great Britain

CONTENTS

INTRODUCTION   6

THE COSTUME   9
    Egyptian   11
    Biblical   17
    Babylonian and Assyrian 17
    Persian   20
    Hebrew   24
    Ancient Greek   28
    Roman   36
    Byzantine and Romanesque 45

STAGE PROPERTIES   58
    Soldiers   58
    Musical instruments   73
    Jewellery   73
    Dress accessories   73
    Furniture   75
    Domestic and religious utensils 77

THE SCENIC DESIGN   84
    Architectural forms   84

STAGE LIGHTING   92

CHOOSING A PLAY   93

INDEX   95

INTRODUCTION

This is the first volume in a series of books about costumes and settings for historical plays. The series is intended for all those who have an interest in and enthusiasm for period drama, whether they are involved with costumes, stage properties, stage design, lighting, or as actors. The main purpose of this book is to suggest to the designer of the historical theatre, costumes and stage settings suitable for plays of the Classical period which can be reproduced effectively in the simplest and most practical way.

The history of costume is so complex and has such a wealth of detail that it is only possible to allude briefly to the relationship between costume and the social customs of each period and nationality. However, an understanding of social history is most important if the interplay of man and environment is to be portrayed accurately. Theatre costume, like fashion itself, is part of that environment, developing out of primitive rituals and dances. These expressed religious beliefs, aggressive attitudes and historical legends which were acted out in dance and song. Elaborate costumes were an important accompaniment to the free development of dramatic expression and self-confidence.

Costume therefore assumed various forms according to man's intention; the way he appeared to others determined their attitudes and reactions. Characterisation through historical costume must be developed in such a manner as to express visually the actor's personality; the various elements must be carefully chosen in order to contribute harmoniously to the overall effect, giving depth and meaning to the character.

Familiarity with historical data is essential as each costume is a sign of an epoch. Pictures of Egyptian, Greek and Roman figures show that the Ancients followed a fashionable silhouette. In Pharonic Egypt, for example, the triangle was the dominant visual form; it is to be found in the stiff fronts of the royal loin cloths and in some white linen pleated dress

Egyptian male cloth wig cover

6

Greek girl in Doric chiton with kolpos and over-fold

Scenic mask

ornaments. In Greece, fashion reflected the styles of the various architectual Orders: the straight lines of the Doric Column, incurved of the Ionic order, and the rich ornamentation of the Corinthian capital. Byzantine was characterised by a highly decorative spirit, the complex patterns of which were reflected in the architecture. It is interesting to see in the Romanesque how the kingly posture of sitting cross-legged influenced the design of the curule chair of antiquity.

Depending on the period he wishes to represent, the costumier-cum-designer must follow the three basic primitive principles: social rank, occupation and sex-attraction. Women's clothes follow the seduction principle; the object is to attract the opposite sex by the display of feminine charm and is typical of Egyptian costume and some later periods. Dress must also show personal or social rank, differentiating between royalty, nobility and the lower classes. Other costumes are strictly utilitarian, determined by the requirements of occupation or the need for protection against the rigors of climate.

Colours in this early period were naturally somewhat limited, especially in the bright colour range, as most were made from mineral or vegetable dyes. The prevalance of indigo shows that for several centuries it remained the most esteemed and widely used dye. Jewellery was worn throughout all periods from the Egyptian to the Romanesque and was highly decorative and exquisite, sometimes exceeding present-day jewellery both in design and workmanship. A brief study of past styles of ornamentation in the local museum would, without doubt, improve historical costume design.

Architecture is as important as costume; both reflect the modes and attitudes of society. Successful scenic design is based upon a sound appreciation of the visual effects of carefully chosen architectural sets which reinforce the style of a production. The set is a combination of static scenery pieces, furniture of the period and the general paraphernalia of stage dressing, and must be designed to allow free movement of the cast. Scenic design has a specific function as a practical support or background to the play and the display of the costumes. The design must, therefore, convey the correct atmospheric impression; it must establish the mood or theme of the play. The theatre, more than any other artistic media, is larger than life. Any design, regardless of its artistic merit, will make little or no impact on the spectator if it remains commonplace. Both set design and costume design must

7

Bacchus mask

Scenic mask

Scenic mask

emphasise the spirit of a performance but they must be kept subordinate to the play itself.

The technique of stage lighting should not be overlooked in the final composition. Stage lighting is used to complement costume and scenic effects, for without it the visual effect of the production will be poor, perhaps even lost. The brief chapter on lighting will, I hope, encourage set designers to familiarise themselves with this important feature.

In this volume I have drawn from a magnitude of information the essential elements of theatrical historical costumes from the Egyptian to the Romanesque periods; unnecessary details have been omitted. It is not the meticulous detail, so important to fashion, but the overall effect which is critical. In simple terms, a theatre costume is the arrangement of materials in such a way as to express the style of a period.

The illustrations have been drawn, as far as it is practical, in clear and simplified way for those not too familiar with 'reading' the beautiful costume designs which are usually created by professional designers and wardrobe experts. The designer, unlike the actor, must find expression not in words or movement but through costume and stage setting.

In the chapter on stage properties I have included all properties. Soldiers and their weapons and armour have been detailed without, I hope, making a complex subject sound even more complex. I have tried to emphasise the art of historical costume, not as a series of disconnected historical episodes but as overlapping styles from period to period. Fighting warriors wore a variety of headdresses, horns, plumes, wings, spikes, feathers — all things to induce fear in the enemy. I have included as many of these as possible in the illustrations, as nothing looks more imposing than a well made plumed helmet.

Jewellery, furniture, domestic and religious utensils have been discussed in their respective periods. Space however does not permit an explanation of how to make these articles although I have mentioned some of the materials that can be used.

THE COSTUME

Phyrgian ladies headdress

Many designers try to develop replicas of historical costume antiques, this is wrong. It is better to design these costumes by suggesting different characteristics of the period. Take the general silhouette of the particular period required, add the proper representative colour and suggest the ornamentation.

It may be difficult not to look at historical costume as pageantry and so focus all the attention to the garment at the expense of the actor; but put aside the temptation. The actor belongs there with both his interior and exterior reality, a thinking being, creator of values, endowed with a particular form of appearance. Remember that actors and actresses are individuals and must be dressed as such. Costume should be designed with a sense of movement of the body; no action should be impeded.

To have a better sense of costume construction, use a lay-figure or a fashion doll. Make a pattern from the measurements of a human figure; pattern shapes are determined by the different parts of the body and the ultimate design of the costume. For an experiment, take a piece of material, drape it over the lay-figure, pin and cut directly on the figure. Trace the result on squared paper.

Obviously the choice of material is important in costume making. All materials are different, in their pliability and the way they fall. However, most kinds can be used. Unbleached calico, muslin, cambric, wool jersey, velveteen and other common type fabrics with the proper dyeing and lighting, can all be made to represent the more expensive materials. Under good lighting conditions rough textured materials give better effects than the smoother textured ones.

The dyeing of materials should be done under the same lighting conditions as those of the stage, so as to become a part of the overall colour scheme of the scene. Excellent dyes are available from all good haberdashery counters. Remember to test each textile to see the reaction of the dye, and try

9

Grecian fan of feathers

different methods: tie-dyeing, dye-bath, batik, spraying, stencilling, and take the best result. Colour and material recommendations are given for all the periods covered in this volume.

Colours   In Egypt white was predominant for both bleached and unbleached fabrics, but with the use of mineral dyes, and later vegetable dyes and indigo, the range of colours increased giving shades of red, yellow, terracotta, green and black. Geometric designs were popular. Materials were fabrics of both a coarse and fine texture, usually linen, wool, transparent linen, or fine linen embroidered with gold, silver and purple. Animal skins were also worn and sandals of leather and fibre.

The colours of the Babylonian, Assyrian and Persian costumes were similiar to those of the Egyptian.

The Hebrews differed in their strongly contrasting multi-coloured costumes made in linen, silk, fine muslin, wool, or camel or goat's hair in shades of red, purple, green, and yellow, with broad black and brown stripes.

The Greeks used a variety of colours ranging from blue-black, blue-green, white, yellow-green, violet, indigo, and light blue made of soft linen, silk, geometric patterned fabric, and semi-transparent woven fabric with gold and silver thread. The white toga was the national dress of the Romans and colours followed their vocations and class for example, purple and crimson for the upper class, subdued colours for peasants, green for the doctors, blue for the philosopher, and purple for the army generals. Apart from white, women wore scarlet, blue, yellow, and green. The typical materials were linen, wool, and silk with embroidered borders.

The Byzantine era was an age of brilliance, with colours of purple, white, green, black, grey, brown, blue, red and wine. The fabrics were of silk, damask, velvet, brocade, tapestry, linen and wool.

The Romanesque period had brighter shades of reds, greens, purple, yellow and brown. Typical materials were animal skins, leather, heavy fabric, home spun hemp, linen, wool, silk, brocade, and transparent fabrics.

Egyptian Queen with vulture
headdress and broad decorated
collar. The dress is full and made
from a fine material secured
by a broad high waist belt and
sash drawing the material to the
front. The Egyptian King figure
wearing the double crown of
Egypt has a full robe over
close-fitting long under tunic.
An ornamented sash pleated in
the front, a broad highly decorated collar and sandals with
turned-up toe-pieces

Egyptian

The costume of the Egyptians was simple and decorative
revealing the figure, both in the draped and undraped styles.
The construction was simple and drapery, when present, was
placed in the front. Basically men and women were dressed
similarly, but there was, as always in early costumes, a subtle
difference. Because of climatic conditions the garments were

Red crown of Lower Egypt

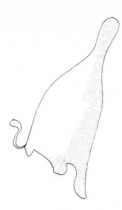

White crown of Upper Egypt

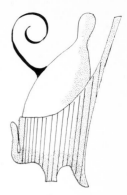

Double crown of Egypt

made of cotton or linen; the upper class often wore a fine transparent muslin. Although coloured garments were worn, white was predominent, this being enriched with coloured embroidered borders and edgings. Colours ranged from blues, yellows, greens, black and purple. In reality these were pastel shades because of the dyes available, but 'stage licence' is allowed by making these colours strong and bright.

Men in earlier times were often scantily dressed, the principal item of clothing being the schenti (loin cloth). This was a long piece of material which was wound round the hips and secured by a belt. The rank or importance of the wearer was shown by the finish, the slave being very simply dressed. The high dignitaries wore the schenti with a pleated apron down the front, often coloured and ornamented. The more elaborate clothing of the Pharoah and dignitaries of an official nature were long and draped. In the later period the skirt was longer, much fuller and stiffer than the schenti, which could be either with a box-type pleat in the front or wound round tight at the back, then drawn up to the centre front and allowed to fall in drapes from the waist. The girdle for the skirt could be made of material which was wound round the hips or by an ornamental waist belt from which was suspended a triangular ornamented piece, often made from leather and decorated with metal studs or shapes. With the skirt the upper part of the body was bare.

The tunic was a simple garment with short sleeves similar to a kimono. The round neck had a slit in front to enable it to be put on over the head. The length from knee to ankle

A member of the Royal Household in a wig, and a sheath close-fitting gown supported by one shoulder strap, and a broad beaded collar. An Egyptian female attendant wearing a wig with a perfumed cone on top, and a fillet. The transparent dress is draped from one shoulder, also a beaded collar

13

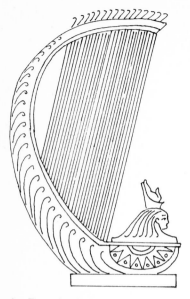

An Egyptian harp

varied, and it could have a waist belt or remain unbelted. It was made in heavy or transparent linen or of a very soft fabric.

The long robe was fuller and most graceful. It was rectangular with a centre hole for the head, being sewn up under the arms from the bottom hem to chest level forming an opening for the sleeves. The drapes were often drawn up to the front. A broad waist girdle was usually worn, but if not, then the robe was allowed to fall straight down revealing a long tunic beneath. The rectangular shaped piece of fabric was draped around the body in various positions and was known as a shawl.

Beards   The Egyptians were usually clean shaven but high dignitaries, including the Pharoahs, on ceremonial occasions, wore a postiche (a false beard) attached by a chin strap. This was of a slim cylindrical shape, 15 cm long (6 in.), and hung from the tip of the chin.

The *hair* was usually black and wavy. That worn by slaves was the round bob which was cut in overlapping layers. This developed into a popular style for nearly all classes, exposing the ears and being cut longer at the back. Wigs were much in evidence and came in various lengths and thicknesses, and they were dyed in various shades of blue and red. Apart from the wigs which were sometimes covered with a painted cloth, the *headdresses* of the royal family were very ornate and are shown on page 12.

Footwear   Turned-up sandals were worn.

Women   Women wore high waisted tunics which hung from under the breasts and draped from between them, falling to calf length or ground level. The wrap-around skirt was worn by slaves, sometimes without a top piece, but often with a short three-quarter circular cape which covered the neck, shoulders and breasts. The two versions of the woman's tunic were distinct from one another. The first type followed the style of the men with the wide kimono sleeves and the centre opening to go over the head, the popular version was the sleeveless type which hung under the breasts and was supported by either a single shoulder strap or wide straps over each shoulder. There was often a deep collar as well. The close fitting robe followed the male style with the

14

A high priestess dressed in a
long robe with a small fringed
cape covering the shoulders.
She is carrying her sistrum and
anointing oil. The slave fan-
bearer has a head cloth and
dressed in a knee-length robe
with the fullness forming large
sleeves, the lower section gathered at the waist in a knot

Queen's headdress

exception of the high waist line. The material was usually soft, giving an easy draping effect in the characteristic style of a centre radiation from the front.

Normally the *hair* hung long over the shoulders, the ends finishing in tight ringlets. The rich ladies wore wigs of often coloured hair. Women added to *headdresses* anything from simple ribbon fillets to the elaborate pieces used by dignitaries and the royal family. Sometimes a single cone shape, some 10 to 15 cm (4 to 6 in.) high, held perfumed ointment. Like the men, the women also wore wigs which were covered with painted or decorated cloth. The ornaments which adorned the headdresses were significant of rank; the royal uraeus, the lotus, the asp. A queen may wear the sacred feather or the isis, and the crowns of the Upper and Lower Nile. Characteristic was the royal stiff tall hat with uraeus and painted fillet.

With *make-up* these dark skinned ladies used lighter shades to make themselves fairer than their male counterparts. They used kohl (charcoal) over the blue eye shadow, round the eyes, continuing outwards to the sides of the face. The lips were rouged in carmine and the cheeks were made pink. Both fingers and toes were treated with orange henna.

Footwear   The sandals were either of the oriental style with turned-up toes, or the plaited type painted and with metal ornamentations.

There was a great extravagance in *jewellery*, and both sexes wore necklaces, bracelets, pendants, earrings and jewelled belts, all highly coloured. Umbrellas and fans of papyrus or feathers were carried, usually just by the slaves, for the protection of their masters.

Children in all the early periods of history wore small editions of the adult costume.

Ornaments   A popular accessory by both male and female was the large collar. This was flat and round and stretched from the base of the neck to the shoulders and was deep to the chest, being made of either beads or soft wire and blended into patterns. Also worn was an ornament of gold and enamel which hung on a gold chain over the collar, this was called

Egyptian hand mirror

Female cloth wig cover

a pectoral, and was worn only by high dignitaries and the royal family. Other necklaces were made from shells and semi-precious stones.

Dressing of *soldiers* for these times was simple. They were provided with a broad band of protective leather which covered the chest to the waist. Often this was supported by shoulder straps, and metal studs decorated the leather. This was worn over the tunic. Weapons carried were daggers, swords, battle axes, spears and bows and arrows. For fuller details see the section on Stage properties.

Biblical

In this chapter for biblical and religious plays the peoples involved are mainly the Hebrews, Assyrians, Babylonians and Persians. Climatically they dressed similarly, with the emphasis on woollen and animal skin garments in contrast to the Egyptians who were more lightly clad.

The costumes remained simple in structure, consisting of two types of garment: a straight tunic or candys, and a shawl. Varying designs and application were present throughout the period. Both male and female wore variations of these garments. Linen, although used, was not so popular as wool or dressed-leather skins.

Babylonian and Assyrian

The *men's* tunics, both long and short, were cut to suit the persuit of the wearer. Popular was the knee length type tunic and for horse riding an inverted V-shape was inserted in the front. Garments are in most cases depicted with fringes, a seemingly popular fashion. The upper class male wore a close fitting broad belt in a cumberband style, over which was a narrower belt. The majority of men wore just a simple narrow leather belt.

The shawl was draped over the left shoulder drawn across the back under the right arm and then further thrown over

the left shoulder, allowing the end to drape down the back. Narrower shawls were normally worn only by high dignitaries and kings. They were made of a large rectangular shaped piece, fringed on the leading edges and then folded and attached to a cord at the waist. The shawl was then placed over the right shoulder and over the back of the left shoulder, over the elbow of the left arm, across the body and then wrapped round the waist under the right elbow, and then fastened in front, left of the waist. The drapery was then contained by another cord or belt.

Beards and moustaches were fashionable and most grown men wore them. The beards were long to mid-chest usually thick and curly and cut off square at the bottom. Because of their elaborate nature either a great deal of time must have been spent on them or they were false.

Hair, as was usual for people from these parts, was black and bushy. The shoulder length style was dressed behind the ears and finished with a straight fringe over the forehead. The almost symetrical set waves and curls again must have made a great deal of work unless a wig was worn. Others allowed their hair to be natural and sometimes wore simple headbands. A simple hat, fez shaped, and for royalty a high domed turban draped with a soft material, was often worn.

Jewellery was worn by both sexes, this being in the main earrings, rings, bracelets, armlets and crowns. Mirrors and ivory combs were very common. Umbrellas, fans and fly whisks were usually manipulated and carried by slaves, for the convenience of their masters.

Footwear   Bare feet were common practice, but sandals and soft skins could be worn. For soldiers and hunting a higher laced leather boot was sometimes worn.

Soldiers wore chain mail over their tunics which reached to just below the knees, but could on occasions be ankle length. A cross belt or baldrick was worn from the right shoulder to the left hip. Daggers were carried on the right in the belt. Shields of various shapes were also carried. Metal helmets were worn, pointed, crested or round.

The *women's* costume differed very slightly from that of

An Assyrian Officer with armoured breast plates over a knee-length kalasiris. He has a large standing shield. His legs are covered with a gaiter-type leg and foot covering

An Assyrian nobleman wearing a to the ground under-garment with a long fringed stole which is wrapped round the body. He is wearing the truncated cone hat. His hair and beard being tightly curled

19

their male counterparts. The tunic was long to the ankles, sleeves were to elbow length, the high round collar was similar to the men's, and the tunic was worn without a girdle. The upper class ladies usually wore a jewelled neck collar around the throat. Like the males, the ladies wore the rectangular shawl, this was fringed on one long side only. It was then held in position on the left hip. It was wrapped around the back, under the right arm, across the front, round to the back again and under the right arm, then in a diagonal direction across the front and placed over the left shoulder across the back. The ends were then draped over the right shoulder. The fringe as in the men's decoration, was an indispensable part of the costume.

Persian

The Persian costume plays many parts in both biblical and Greek drama.

The *men's* prevailing feature was the tunic which differed from the Assyrian in that it had long, tight sleeves to the wrists. It fitted close to the body and was often worn without a belt. It could be knee length, but sometimes was calf to ankle length. Under the tunic were worn close-fitting pantaloons down to the ankles. A robe, similar to the Egyptian's, was worn with the coat which came in two styles. The ankle length style was without fastenings and open down the front. It had straight sleeves with turned-back cuffs. At the neck was a turned-back collar with a simple ribbon fastening. The shorter knee length style of coat had cut-away skirts and wrapped over the front and was secured by a belt. It had no collar or cuffs.

The Persian's *hair* was black, but cut shorter than the Assyrian style, with the ears exposed. It was full and fashioned in small tight curls.

Headdresses The headbands were often of twisted cloth worn low over the forehead. Another style was a high fillet shaped crown with a feather decoration. A hood was the most popular style of headdress and strikingly different from the

A Persian lady in a fringed draped shawl and a head-covering with hanging gold ornaments

The man is wearing the kandys which is gathered in the front and sides and secured at the waist. The sleeves full to the waist being wide at the wrist but narrower at the arm-holes

costumes of the Babylonians, Assyrians and the Hebrews. It was worn by soldiers, huntsmen and servants. Basically it was a loose cloth which framed the face, often concealing the lower jaw. There were variations, some with peaks and some without. Soldiers usually wore the peakless variety which stood high and stiff with ribbons hanging down the back. This was

The young lady is wearing the
typical Persian dress of the
period which was a long rectangular piece of material wrapped
round the body

The man is wearing the Median
costume of the long full kandys
gown, which was gathered at the
front, sides and hitched up at
the waist. The hood covered
the head surrounding the face
and chin

A Persian High Priest in the
long Median style

A soldier dressed in the Median
style — a deep leather cap with
long side flaps often long enough
to be tied under the chin. The
coat varied from neck to either
thigh or knee length with close
fitting sleeves. Breeches reached
either to the knees or to the
ankles

a Mede fashion, but Persian soldiers wore this in battle. They carried swords, daggers, javelins, bows and shields. Walking sticks were popular and carried by most upper-class men.

Jewellery, although worn, was less evident. Earrings, rings and jewelled collars were worn by both sexes.

The Persian *women's* dress, although following the Babylonian and Assyrian fashion cannot be too accurate as few records exist of such garments, but for all stage costume purposes it must be assumed they followed the tunic style of the Assyrians.

Footwear   Bare feet were frequent in slaves and the ordinary people, but footwear generally followed the fashion of soft leather shoes often with turned-up points.

Colours followed closely the Egyptians and the Assyrians, the dyeing processes being identical.

Hebrew brimmed cap

Hebrew fringed pointed cap

Hebrew

Being basically desert people the dress of the Hebrews followed the styles of the wrap around garments that protected them from the heat, sun, and sand. They were decorated with broad perpendicular stripes.

Resembling the style of the Assyrians, the *men* wore ankle length tunics, often fringed round the hem, short sleeved and worn with a shawl. Later two tunics were worn, one over a close sleeved ankle length tunic, the other a long caftan decorated with fringes along the edges. A robe, called the aba, similar to the earlier Egyptian garment was worn. The aba, shawl and caftan had tassels at each corner, always in purple. These tassels represented the four consonants of the Holy Name, JeHoVaH.

The dark *hair* was worn semi-long, usually waved and curled and higly glossed with oil. *Beards* were worn by most Hebrew men, and left long and neatly trimmed.

The general silhouette of the Egyptian costume revealed the figures in their
simply constructed garments. A suggested setting are huge round columns as
a background

Characteristic of the Greek costumes are the rectangular pieces of material draped over the body, made in various styles, such as the Doric and Ionic chiton. Pillars were much in evidence in Greek times and make suitable backgrounds for all Greek plays

Hebrew High Priest (Rabbi) in robe decorated with pomegranites and real bells
Hebrew lady wearing a voluminous cloak

Headdresses   The headcloth with the twisted cord was popular with the shepherd community, but the pointed cap, similar to the Babylonians, Persians and Assyrians, was often worn, likewise small caps with earflaps. The Pharisees wore turbans with rounded tops and drapery down the back.

Priests wore ankle-length tunics with long close fitting sleeves, usually made of white linen. Over these was a knee length deep blue robe, with pomegranates embroidered around the hem in blue, scarlet and purple in between which were attached small golden functional bells. Over the robe was placed an apron with shoulder straps. The apron was coloured violet, purple and scarlet in perpendicular stripes and was

25

A young Hebrew girl with nose-ring and 'drum' headwear covering the ears. She is wearing a plain shift dress. The man is wearing the Nomad costume of scarf head covering and full outer garment in the National colours — black and white

Hebrew pointed soft cap

Hebrew tall pleated cap

fringed at the hem. Wrapped around the waist was a girdle of woven linen in the ritual colours mentioned above. A rectangular pouch, in the same material as the apron and decorated with four rows of jewels, was attached to the chest by rings and chains. On the head was worn a high, blue mitre, placed over a white turban. On the mitre was a gold plate on which was engraved Hewbrew characters.

The simple dress of the women was the ankle-length tunic which was sleeveless and loose fitting with a girdle round the waist. The perpendicular design remained in fashion for both male and female throughout the period. Also worn was the robe similar to the male dress with long pointed open sleeves. The robe reached to the ground and was often girdled. Over this was sometimes worn a voluminous cloak-like garment.

The *hair* was usually heavily plaited and made in elaborate braids hung with gold ornaments. The head was always covered either by high or low close-fitting caps and by a scarf head covering, or by fine netting.

Jewellery was worn only by the women, these being rings, bracelets, necklaces, earrings and nose rings.

Sandals were worn.

Children wore clothes similar to their elders, both sexes usually wore a small cap and simple tunics.

Hebrew cooling fan

27

Ancient Greek

From the seventh century BC the pure Greek costume was portrayed through sculptures and writings giving a pictorial history of its development. There were two basic styles for men and women, both depending on drapery and not on shaping or fitting. First was the Dorian, then later, the Ionian.

The Doric chiton, also called the peplos, was the earlier style rectangular-shaped garment, and reached from the shoulder to the ground. Wrapped round the figure, the neck piece and armholes were formed in the fold over.

The Ionic chiton of oriental origin, made of linen, was the masculine garment. After the archaic period it was short to knee length. When the girdle was adjusted the garment was bloused over, and drawn up to mid-thigh length. Often it was secured only on the left shoulder by a fibula (pin) or by knotting the material. Both shoulders could be fastened by pinning or sewing. The longer chiton was now old-fashioned but was still worn by older men, musicians and charioteers. The two over garments could be worn with the chiton or by themselves. The chlamys, a short outer garment, was often worn by horsemen, travellers and soldiers. It was rectangular, of woven wool, and fastened on the right shoulder or at the throat, usually with a brooch or clasp. The himaton, also of a woven material, was wrapped around the body from under the arm on the left side, across the back diagonally to the left shoulder then down over the arm and across the body, up over the right arm to the right shoulder. It crossed the back draping the end over the left arm.

Hair   In the earlier period men wore their hair long in curls or gathered at the back in a knot. The Spartans wore long hair for a much longer period than the Athenians. Later it was considered to be effeminate, and short hair became the fashion. *Beards* also became unfashionable with older men and intellectuals and when worn were usually without a moustache and were stiff and pointed.

Headdresses   Fillets or wreaths were worn around the head, but a simple cap similar to the Hebrew's headgear was popular. The large petasos (sun hat) with a slightly pointed crown and

Helmet with a fixed visor

28

A Greek goddess dressed in a piplose with a girdle above the overfold. She is wearing the Phrygian helmet

The figure above is wearing the chiton with a double girdle

29

The Greek soldier is wearing a corselet of leather with small overlapping metal plates with shoulder pieces. The lower body was protected by strips of leather called 'Pteruges'. The Doric-style helmet is being carried

The lady is wearing the chiton with himitation draped around the head

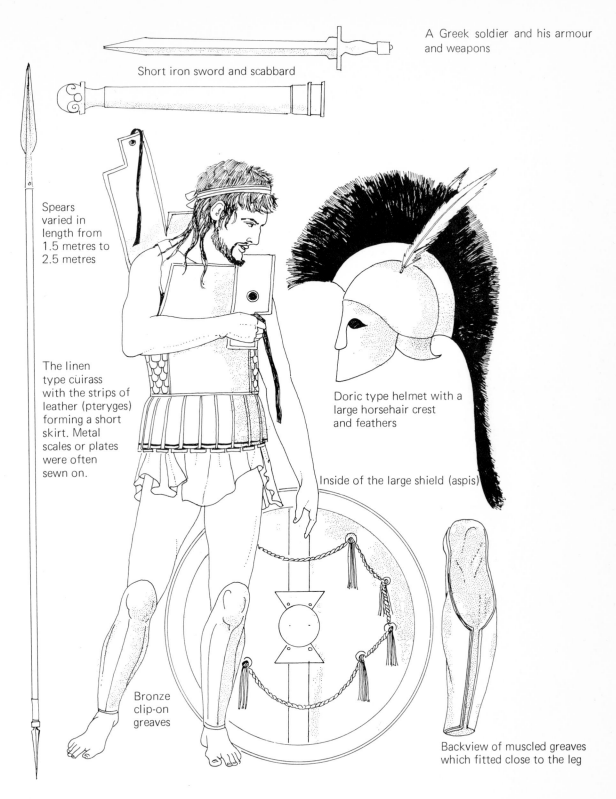

Short iron sword and scabbard

A Greek soldier and his armour and weapons

Spears varied in length from 1.5 metres to 2.5 metres

The linen type cuirass with the strips of leather (pteryges) forming a short skirt. Metal scales or plates were often sewn on.

Doric type helmet with a large horsehair crest and feathers

Inside of the large shield (aspis)

Bronze clip-on greaves

Backview of muscled greaves which fitted close to the leg

31

Greek ladies headdress

Phyrgian shield

Greek sword

a wide brim was worn by travellers. The Phrygian cap was sometimes worn.

Soldiers are best shown wearing the chiton under a cuirass of leather with overlapping small metal plates and a helmet with a plume. The legs were covered with greaves or shin guards of brass. Weapons were spears, javelins, short swords, leather sling shots and bows and arrows. See Stage Properties section.

The *women's* basic garment was the Doric peplos (chiton) usually made of wool and very plain, much favoured by the women of Sparta. Fastened on the shoulders by a fibula (pin), both front and back were so arranged that it made a high straight at the back and fell into drooping folds in the front. This excess of material which was an essential feature of the Doric chiton, was allowed to overhang giving a blouse effect, this was called the kolpos. In the very simplest of forms the peplos was worn without a girdle and the side was left open. There were however many variations, eg the open side could be sewn from the waist to the hem and the fullness was then passed through a girdle thus giving an effect of a blouse and skirt. Another belt was often worn over the girdle — the fullness furthering the impression of two garments known as the *peplos of Athena*. The overlapping style was the Ionic chiton. Although similar in construction, it was made of thin linen or even transparent silk. Made from a rectangular piece of material, but with a great fullness which made it necessary to use more pins to fasten the top edge, an open seam on either side of the neck, down each arm to form elbow length sleeves, was made. As it was shorter than the peplos there was no blousing effect and being of softer material it was often girdled just below the bust, but many girdle variations were introduced. The length of the skirt was also adjustable, higher for huntresses and girl atheletes. The tops of the garments were often sewn rather than pinned. Sometimes the Ionic chiton was used as an under garment with the Doric chiton worn open on top. The outer garment worn during the period was the himaton which was wrapped around the body passing under the left arm then pinned to the right shoulder. The fullness draped down the right arm being secured by pins like the sleeves of the Ionic chiton. Also the method of wrapping the material behind the back allowed the loose ends to drape over the forearms.

Young Greek lady fastening her Doric chiton with a brooch or a clasp over her Ionic dress A Greek soldier in a travelling cloak and hat

A Greek citizen wearing the himitation worn here as the only main garment. It was simply a length of material made of heavy cotton or wool and draped around the lower body, leaving the upper part and arms bare

Lady wearing the Ionic chiton.
The top edge of the garment
was fastened along the shoulders
and arms with clasps

Armed with a spear and
wickerwork shield (Pelta)

Ear flaps hanging

The Phrygian cap

Ear flaps pulled and tied back

Back view

A Thracian Peltast (a mercenary)

Greek comedian wearing a mask. The Greeks employed masks in the theatre, mainly that a few actors could take several parts, merely by changing their masks.

The mouthpiece of the Greek theatrical masks amplified the voice of the actor. The masks were designed with exaggerated features and expressions

Sandals or bare feet were adopted for both male and female.

The earlier *hairstyle* for women was ringlets, thin snake-like curls which were held in place by fillets or wreaths. Later, and the most popular style, was the neatly tied back variety with the knot or chignon carefully made at the back of the neck and held in place by a fillet or a band. The hair was usually undecorated but hairpins were used. The Greeks were naturally fair, but they made use of dyes and wigs. Head coverings were made of a variety of nets, veils, kerchiefs, and the large petasos (sun hats) worn by the men.

Jewellery was used in moderation, the men confined themselves to rings, whilst the women wore bracelets, necklaces, earrings, rings, brooches and ornamented pins (fibulae)

Children when they emerged from their swaddling clothes, were dressed very simply. Boys wore the chlamys and girls the simple Ionic chiton. After eleven or twelve they were dressed in clothes resembling the adults.

Ladies carried parasols and fans, the men preferred the walking stick.

Roman

It would be impossible to explain all the folding methods of the various togas which was the principal garment of the Romans. They changed continually throughout the Roman civilisation, reflecting the changes of fashion and public tastes. The true toga came in about the sixth century BC, small and not unlike the Greek chlamys. By the first and second centuries AD the size had grown enormously, because of this it was suitable only for the wealthier classes. The toga was, however, the distinguishing garment of the Romans between themselves and the Barbarians, or anyone else in the world. Every Roman citizen had the right to wear this, their true national garb. The toga at first was the only male garment except for a loin cloth, until about 300 BC, when the tunica was introduced and worn as a nether garment.

A Roman general wearing a metal cuirass or breastplate and armoured kilt over his short tunic. Across his shoulder he is wearing a cloak made from a length of heavy woollen cloth fastened on the shoulder and draped over the left arm, leaving the right arm free. The cloak was usually red in colour showing his personal emblem of military command. The head is adorned with the laurel leaf headdress of a victorious general

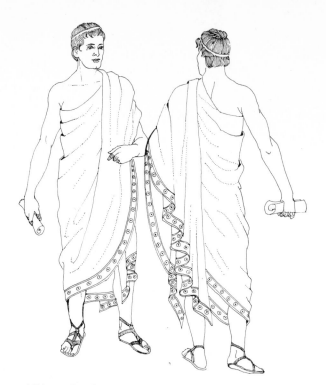

Figures showing the folds of the toga front and back view

Although the toga varied in size from period to period, it also assumed differences of colour and decoration to distinguish classes of the wearer. Here are some examples of the various togas in use.

The pura worn by the ordinary *male* citizen was plain and in a yellowish-white wool material and some 15 cm (6 in.) shorter than the other styles. It was worn on formal occasions, discarded for work. The praetexta was a purple bordered toga donned by officials of public office and oddly enough by boys up to the age of sixteen, of the upper class, who at this age ceremoniously discarded and assumed the virilis toga. The candida was the ordinary pura toga, but bleached whiter, and worn by men searching office. The picta was a purple toga, embroidered with a pattern in gold thread. This was the ceremonial triumphal toga worn by generals. It was the property of the State and later became the traditional costume of the emperors. The pulla toga was usually in a dark colour, brown or black usual for mourning. The tunica, similar to the Greek chiton in its simplest form was made of a woollen material, usually yellowish-white. It was made from two pieces of material, sewn together, leaving a slit at the sides for the arms. This sleeveless type tunica was used by manual workers, and was usually worn off the

Roman boy wearing a toga and hanging round his neck is a bulla

The lady is wearing a toga with a built-up headdress

right shoulder to allow for greater freedom of the arms. A belt was worn around the waist, except informally. It fell to just above the knees and was a little shorter at the back. During the first century AD the tunica sleeves became shaped and longer, first to elbow length, then later wide sleeves developed and by the second and third centuries AD the wide and narrow sleeves became known as dalmatica. The decorations of the tunica were merely ornamentation of class distinction, for the ordinary people they were plain without any form of decoration. A stripe of purple some 4 cm (1½ in.) in depth, the angustus clavus, being down the front and back was the mark of knights, magistrates and other upper class groups.

A garment with a wider purple stripe of about 6 cm (2½ in.), the latus clavus, was worn by senators. Later these decorations ceased to have any significance and their main function was purely decorative.

The tunica palmata was originally worn by victorious generals with the toga picta. This was a magnificent purple garment embroidered with gold thread in motifs of some military campaign. It was the forerunner of the usual dress of the emperors, and later as a sleeved tunic of the magnificent court costumes of the Byzantium.

A Roman general in a toga picta which later became the usual garment of the Emperor
A Roman legionaire wearing the armour and carrying the weapons of the period

Outer garments were generally distinguished by their size and name, as all were rectangular in shape, except perhaps for the paenula which was a semi-circular cloak. The sagum was a practical garment made of a thick woollen material, usually in dark colours. The cloak was wrapped around the body and fastened on the right shoulder. The most popular cloak was the lacerna, which fell to just below hip level and had rounded corners, and which was worn across the shoulders and fastened at the neck or right shoulder by a fibula (pin). The paludamentum, which was similar to the sagum, only larger was the cloak worn by officers, and made of a finer material than the sagum. It was worn over the armour and came in various colours, white, purple and scarlet. The pallium like the himation of the Greeks, was worn mainly by teachers, philosophers and religious teachers. Later this became more popular than the toga.

The paenula was cut in a semi-circular shape and was worn round the shoulders like a South American poncho. It varied from hip to ankle length, either fastened up the front by hooks and eyes, or pins or sewn all the way up with a slit for the head. This was worn by country people and travellers. The birrus and the laena which were mainly worn by the working people, were made with a hood. The cloak was in a thick coarse material.

40

These figures are wearing the toga over the head for inclement weather, front and back view

The *soldiers* wore a rust coloured tunica somewhat shorter than civilian wear. Over this was worn the lorica or cuirass. This came in various designs, cast metal front and back and hinged, worn by officers, either with overlapping scales, iron links, or articulated plates. This armour was usually placed over a short leather jacket which had hanging metal tipped tabs. These tabs hung down to about mid-thigh and down the upper arms. Breeches or shorts were worn, these were close fitting and sometimes hung below the knees. Greaves similar to the Greeks were worn, but the high laced military buskins lined with animal skin, were more usual. The open design caligula boots in various styles, but all coming high over the ankle, were the usual footwear of the soldiers.

The *helmets* were made of iron, some with crests and horsehair plumes, others like the legionaires were plain with metal chin guards.

The *Roman shield*, made from leather which was stretched over a metal frame, was oblong in shape and convex (to protect the whole body). Each different legion had its peculiar device or insignia marked in metal decoration on the shield. The offensive weapons consisted of a sword, a little longer than the Greeks, but still short and thick in an ornamented scabbard. This sword was attached to a sword belt which

41

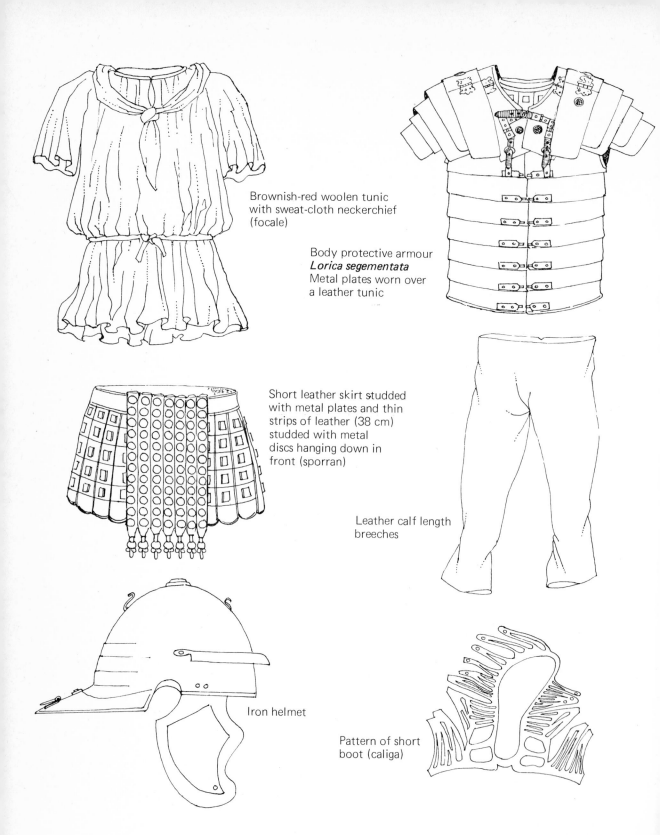

Brownish-red woolen tunic
with sweat-cloth neckerchief
(focale)

Body protective armour
Lorica segementata
Metal plates worn over
a leather tunic

Short leather skirt studded
with metal plates and thin
strips of leather (38 cm)
studded with metal
discs hanging down in
front (sporran)

Leather calf length
breeches

Iron helmet

Pattern of short
boot (caliga)

was slung diagonally from the right shoulder to the left hip. Long spears and javelins were carried.

Standard bearers wore the usual uniform with the distinguishing difference of an animal skin over his head instead of a helmet. They bore the badges of companies, a spread-winged eagle holding a thunderbolt in its claws was the symbol which topped the standard pole.

Roman men wore their *hair* comparitively short, but it was crimped with irons and perfumed, with short curls on the forehead and at the nape of the neck. *Beards* were worn during the periods, but they had only short vogues. If worn they were usually short and close cut. To be smooth shaven was possibly the main fashion throughout.

Roman *women* wore a long undergarment, tunica interior, made usually of soft linen. Oven this was the basic garment, the stola which was worn throughout the period and was similar in style to the Ionic chiton. The stola being fuller than the tunica had the sleeves taken from the fullness of the material, it was always long, covering the instep. The stola either hung straight or was draped in a variety of ways with girdles, and was made of soft wool or soft linen. Over the stola was worn a palla as an outer garment, this being an adaption of the Greek himation and draped in a similar fashion.

The *boys* like their fathers wore the tunica, their station in life being marked with the clavi which his class permitted. After sixteen they wore the toga praetexta. Around their necks they wore a locket or bulla from infancy. For the rich the bulla was of gold, for the ordinary boys it was made of leather. It was a hollow hinged ornament which contained an amulet. This was discarded at the age of sixteen.

The *girl's* garment usually consisted of a simple tunica or Greek type chiton.

Hair The development of the Roman women's coiffure was very complex. The earlier styles followed closely that of the Greeks, but from the latter era of the Republic they became very elaborate. The hair was dyed or bleached and false pieces of blonde or red hair were often used. The hair was braided and coiled, frizzed with elaborate curling and

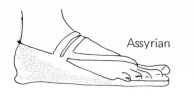 Assyrian

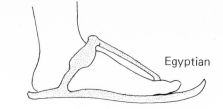 Egyptian

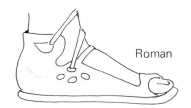 Roman

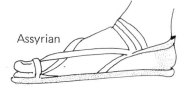 Assyrian

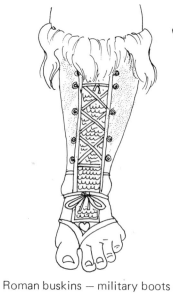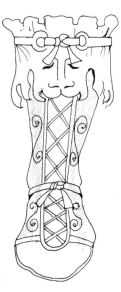

Roman buskins — military boots

 Greek

 Greek

Roman

Shoes

high build-ups in the front. A fashionable style was for the hair to be built into a high cone on top of the head which was supported by a metal frame. Veils were used prefusely with many of the coiffures.

The Romans of both sexes usually went bare headed, although for special occasions a variety of headwear was worn. For travellers, the Greek type petasos, and the freed slave pileus, hoods and portions of the toga were worn.

Footwear Women, similar to the men, wore soleae in the home and calcei outdoors.

Colours were red, yellow, white and green.

Byzantine and Romanesque

Most characteristic feature of the Byzantine costume was colour, as was also apparent in their jewellery. The influence of both Greco-Roman and Oriental mysticism emerged in the costume alongside of the new-found Christianity.

Byzantine *men* wore a long straight under garment with long tight sleeves. The over tunic was similar in cut to the Roman tunica, the sleeves in one with the garment. The length varied from just below the knees to almost ground level. High dignitaries wore a richly embroidered mantle, a loose sleeved tunic or dalmatica. The legs were covered in breeches or braccae, reminicent of the Roman soldiers, but all men wore some kind of hose, which were close fitting to the legs.

The cloak was now part of the essential dress, being worn indoors as well as out. The simplest form was the rectangular piece of fabric as from the Roman times and worn round the shoulders falling to ground length, fastening at the right shoulder with a brooch. The more formal wear was a semi-circular cape or cope. This fastened also at the right shoulder with an ornamental brooch. Another type of cloak was the circular cape similar to the Roman paenula, this was sewn up at the front with a slit for the head. This style was often fitted with a detatchable hood.

Workers wore breeches tucked into knee length boots.

A Byzantine noble gentleman
wearing a rectangular cloak
ornamented with a 'tablion' an
oblong panel richly embroidered
A Byzantine lady of high birth
with a jewelled headdress and
wearing the 'lorum' symbolic of
the toga picta

Over this was worn a thigh-length loose sleeved tunic and an ankle length cloak.

Soldiers were dressed similarly to that of the later Roman legionaires, the helmet now being with a deeper brim.

Men's *hair* altered little in style, being cut short or bobbed with a fringed band across the forehead. *Beards* and moustaches, when worn, were neatly trimmed.

Hats also changed little, there was the sun hat (petasos), the cloak hood and sometimes the Phrygian hat.

Byzantine *women's* costume followed closely that of the menfolk. They wore the long high necked straight tunic or chemise with long sleeves which reached the ankle. It was drawn in at the waist with a girdle. Over this was a tunic which was slightly shorter than the under tunic, thus leaving the edges of the under tunic showing. The over tunic could be girdled or not, according to taste of the wearer.

A veil was often present and draped over the forearm. Like the men they wore cloaks and capes.

Hair The ladies retained the elaborate hair arrangements of the Imperial Roman period. Often the hair was retained under a turban in the Oriental fashion. The ordinary women or working women coiled their hair upon their heads and covered them with modest veils and hoods.

Included in this section must be representation of the Barbaric, Teutonic and Celtic peoples of Western Europe. This is essential for all plays dealing with the early centuries. Although information is a little scarce, what real evidence of costume there is has come from numerous discoveries of garments found in the peat bogs of North-West Germany, Denmark and Holland. These give a fairly good idea and description of the type of clothes worn.

The *men* wore shirt-like smocks or tunics with or without sleeves of hide, leather or a patterned woollen fabric. These tunics had an opening to the chest and came to knee length, being slipped on over the head or sometimes being sewn on one shoulder and the other fastened with a clasp. Under this was worn short breeches with leg-bandages of wool or hide strips bound round the knee and shins, or long ankle-length breeches which were cross-gartered. Cloaks were worn

The Viking woman is wearing a long pleated underdress with rectangular pinafore-type pieces back and front supported by ornamental straps. This married lady wore a knotted head-scarf. She carried a hand-spindle 'distaff'

The Viking warrior in a helmet with a nasal piece. A short tunic with a leather waist belt. The long tight fitting hose was stuffed into soft leather foot-wear

The silhouette of the Romans followed very closely the Greek costumes with the exception of the toga. Ornate marble chairs, typical of the Roman times, make excellent set pieces for Roman plays

The costume outline for the Romanesque period shows great similarity for the male and female dress. A grey stone background suggests the period

Saxon Peasant Dress — The man has a coarse linen hitched-up tunic with sleeves long to the wrist and a leather belt. A short hose with long strips of linen bandage wound round the legs. The Phyrgian type hat was worn. On his feet are rough leather shoes

The woman wears her over-mantle turned up revealing a short undergown. The head-covering is typical of Saxon women

Roman

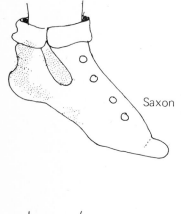

Saxon

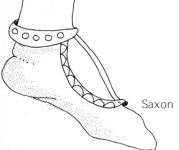

Saxon

Saxon

and cut either semi-circular or rectangular some had hoods attached. Footwear was usually pieces of leather wrapped and laced over the foot.

The men's long *hair* was worn in a braided fashion as was also the *beard* when worn. Large moustaches were sometimes worn without beards and the reverse. Teutonic *women* wore a long skirt with a running draw string, over which was a short tunic similar to the male sleeveless shirt smock. Cloaks were also worn with a rectangular hood.

The *hair* was long and loose to the shoulders until marriage, after which it was braided and drawn up and pinned.

With the intermingling of the Teutonic people and the Roman and Byzantine civilizations, the gradual change to fashion and richer type material took place, especially among the Anglo-Saxons.

The upper class bliant (tunic) was a close fitting garment either laced or sewn up on one or both sides. The sleeves were either long and close-fitting or wide at the top, when the oversleeve was wide it revealed the close sleeve of the under-tunic. The skirt of the bliant varied in length from knee to ankle sometimes being slit at the sides or front or front and back. The skirt was belted at the waist and bloused over the stomach and hips concealing the belt. Under the bliant a man wore short breeches (unseen), but long bracchae (breeches) with or without cross-gartering were also worn.

Stockings were also very popular, these were tailor-made for the upper class, but when made with a coarse heavy fabric for the peasant they appeared clumsy and wrinkled.

The usual outer-garment was the cloak, rectangular, semi-circular or circular, they fastened on either the right or left shoulder with a large fibula. The cloak was sometimes hooded.

Men's *hair* was worn both long and short and in various ways, one Norman fashion was to have the hair shaven at the back level to the ears, the rest cut short and brushed forward. This style was however soon out of fashion and the longer hair-style was more popular, the hair was usually parted in the centre sometimes with a fringe or brushed back. Occasionally long moustaches and *beards* (which were forked) were worn, but more usually the men remained

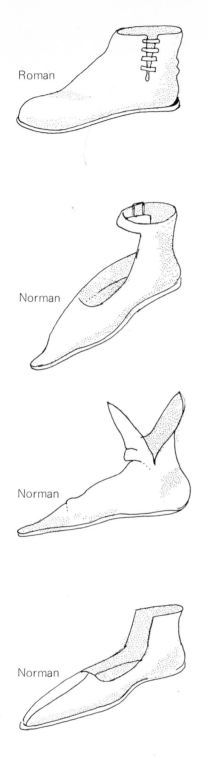

Roman

Norman

Norman

Norman

Shoes

clean-shaven. The fashion of going bare-headed remained in popular usage, but for inclement conditions the head-wear, apart from the hood attached to the cloak, was either the coif-type (bonnet) which fitted over the head like a skull cap, tied under the chin and covered the ears or a pointed cap, similar to the phrygian cap was worn.

Women wore a long under-tunic (chemise) which followed the fit of the overgarment close or loose fitting. The chemise of linen was full length to the ground with a high close neck-line, and long, close sleeves. Over the chemise was worn the shorter looser overgarment with short wide sleeves which revealed the chemise sleeves at the wrist.

The court dress of the bliant style was made in a heavy jersey-type material which fitted very closely to the figure. The skirt part was made from a finer material which fell into fine pleats long to the ground. The sleeves, made from the skirt material, became a characteristic and exaggerated part of the style. The wide cuff became an extreme streamer which was knotted to prevent it trailing on the ground. Similar to the male bliaut the women's bliaut was laced on one or both sides. The girdle which encircled the waist was made of cord, leather or strung metal-discs. The waistline was variable, normal, above or below the hips.

The *hair* was worn long with a centre parting interwoven with ribbons or with ornamental casing of metal cylinders; false hair was often used to supplement any deficiency of normal locks. Later the fashion was to cover the head with a kerchief or wimple.

Jewellery of bracelets, finger-rings, chaplets, belts, belt-buckles, brooches and fibulae were worn.

Clerics Because of the appearance of many characters in clerical garb in the plays of this period a brief analysis of their costume is included.

The main garments of the Benedictine *monks* known as the vestments or habit, consisted of a plain long tunic of white wool (cassock), which fitted over the head and reached the ground. Over this cassock was a loose full black gown to which was attached round the neck a loose cowl or hood. On the feet were plain leather sandals.

The *heads* of the monks was shaven in the style of the

A Saxon soldier wearing a short (byrnie) coat of interlocking iron rings and short sleeves. The tunic underneath has long sleeves and is embroidered round the hem and cuffs. The leg covering was a cross gartered hose. The helmet was of leather reinforced with metal

A Viking soldier in a short tunic also embroidered around the hem and cuffs. The trouser style leg covering reached just above the ankle, the metal helmet had a nasal piece. The beard is plaited

The Anglo-Saxon figure is wearing the knee-length tunic and cross gartered long hose, over his shoulder is a cloak fastened on the right shoulder with a brooch

The Danish soldier has metal plated armour over a short tunic. Long hose were stuffed into fur leggings which were cross gartered. The horned helmet shows him to be a chieftain

A foot soldier wearing the interlocking metal rings hauberk over
a thick padded undercoat

A cavalry soldier wearing the
leather jerkin studded with
metal pieces, which is slit from
the hem to the crotch. He is
wearing the helmet with metal
nose piece and carries the long
kite shaped shield

Norman lady in close fitting bodice and full to the ground skirt with the long dangling exaggerated sleeves tied into a knot. This could be worn with or without a girdle

The Norman style of wearing two tunics one over the other. Over the under tunic is the dolmatic or outer tunic which had wide sleeves and was laced up at the back

The lady is wearing two tunics, one over the other, and a long cape. The head is covered with a close fitting head scarf with fillet

The young man is wearing a short tunic and cross gartered hose, a short cape is fastened from the right shoulder

Celtic monk

Roman tonsure

Monks in their coarse woollen cossacks habits over which was a loose black gown with a hood attached. On the left the monk has the Celtic tonsure and on the right the Roman tonsure

56

Roman tonsure, the crown of the head shaved. This followed the traditional style of the Roman Church from the early centuries and retained by the Byzantine. The pre-Augustinian or Celtic Christians favoured a shaven head with a semi-circular patch in front, from ear to ear. Both these are illustrated.

The ecclesiastical costume of a *bishop* changed very little from this period until the Reformation. It consisted of a white tunic of linen (alb) which was long to the ground, with long loose sleeves, this covered the nether-garment (cassock), and at the hem was a band of embroidery (orphry). A scarf-like length of material (stole), was embroidered and ended in a deep fringe and hung just below the knees. A white linen embroidered collar piece (amice) was tied on with tapes. A girdle of woven linen cord was tied round the waist of the alb. Over this was placed the chasuble a three-quarter circle or oval shape which hung in deep folds. There was also the dalmatic which was shaped like a cross without seams and was placed over the head through a slit at the neck opening. The cope was a full semi-circle of richly decorated material, it was ground length and worn fastened across the chest with large clasps. At the back of the cope hung the cowl. Examples of these copes in velvets, demask and embroidered fabrics can be seen in museums.

Boots or hose were worn at knee length with sandals covering the feet. A low mitre cap highly embroidered was the *headgear* of a bishop.

By this time the bishop carried, or had carried for him, the shepherd crook (crozier) usually made from ivory or ebony.

STAGE PROPERTIES

Stage properties are the finer details incorporated in the final composition of the stage settings. The importance of a property in the action of the play and the overall visual impact cannot be overlooked.

The 'reality' of a play is often judged by the artistic authenticity of the properties. It is indeed a very complex and fascinating part of the art of the theatre. So many different materials and skills are required in the production of properties that an inventive and imaginative mind is required.

The 'props' or property master is theoretically responsible for everything that is moveable on the stage with the exception of the lighting equipment and the scenery. The property department, apart from the furnishing of the set and the general paraphenalia of the stage settings, is also an essential part of the costume, being responsible for all accessories, jewellery and all 'hand' properties. Included in this chapter is the costume of the *soldiers* because the essential parts of the costume have to be made and supplied by the property department. Undoubtedly soldiers play a great part in the periods described in this volume. So a good background knowledge of armourial trappings and weapons of these periods is essential. The many sketches throughout this book will give an idea of their relative size and form.

The ordinary *Egyptian infantry soldier* wore little or no armour; their loin cloth was reinforced with patches of leather. The head covering was a horse-hair or fibre heavy wig. Only the pharaoh and his *corps d'elite* wore a body armour. The pharaoh's armour was in various colours and had a broad enamelled collar which was secured by a golden chain. His kopersh (helmet), had a serpent frontpiece. The units of the *corps d'elite* wore tunics made from several thicknesses of specially treated material.

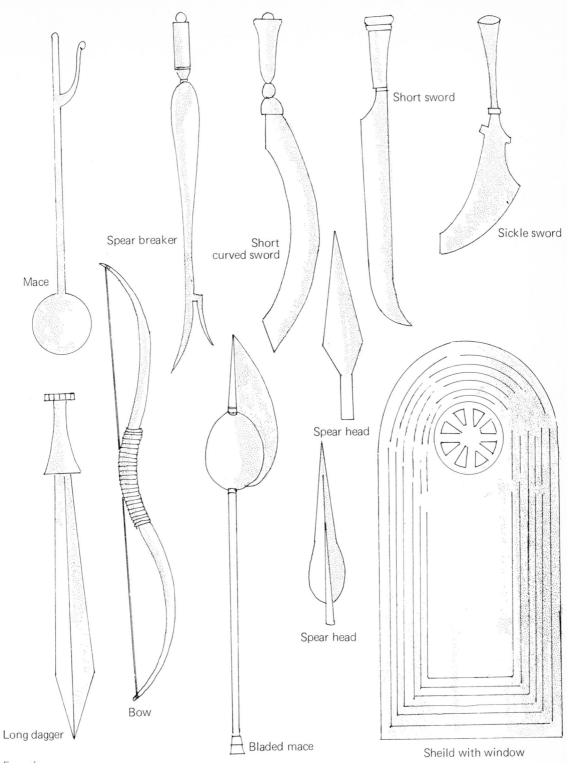

Mace

Spear breaker

Short
curved sword

Short sword

Sickle sword

Spear head

Long dagger

Bow

Bladed mace

Spear head

Sheild with window

Egyptian weapons

59

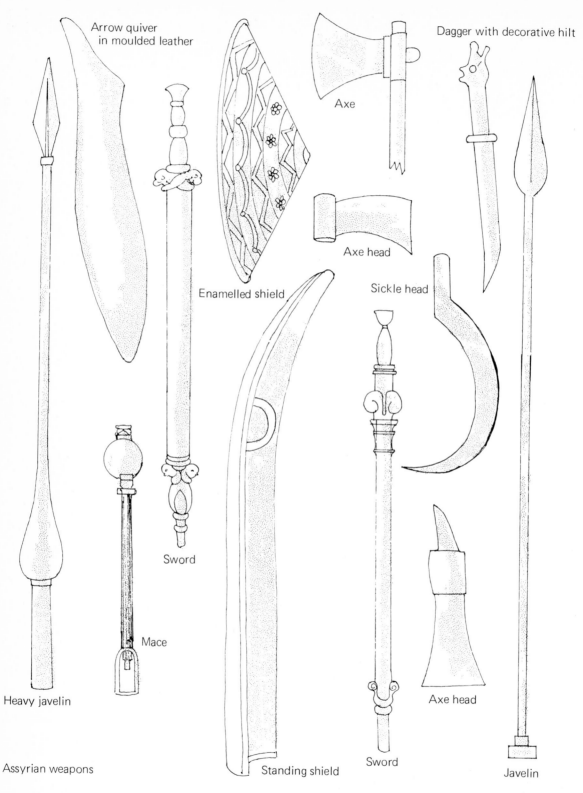

Arrow quiver
in moulded leather

Axe

Dagger with decorative hilt

Axe head

Enamelled shield

Sickle head

Sword

Heavy javelin

Mace

Axe head

Sword

Javelin

Assyrian weapons

Standing shield

60

Pharaoh wearing his gold collar and 'kopersh' headgear for battle

Mercenaries formed a great part of the Egyptian army; many of them were natives of Africa. These conscripts were usually lightly armed with javelins, pikes and slings; their primitive shields were often just painted lengths of wood. Others, the officers, wore coats of crocodile skin and thickly padded leather helmets. They carried an assortment of weapons: swords, daggers and axes.

The *Assyrians* wore close-fitting bronze helmets with pointed or plumed tops and their armour consisted of a primitive chain mail variety or a leather tunic covered with metal plates. The sword was attached from a cross-belt and spears, axes and bows and arrows were carried. The Assyrian soldier paid great attention to his hair and beard, the hair being gathered to the back from a centre parting. Both the moustache and the beard were well groomed and curled. The hair and beard styles have, wherever possible, been drawn with the helmets.

The *Persian soldiers'* dress followed closely that of the Median style with the close fitting tunic and the long close-fitting sleeve to the wrist, under the tunic close-fitting trousers which fitted tightly to the ankle were worn. They wore various types of headgear, called tiaras, some of compressed felt and others were made of leather and the helmets were made from bronze. Corselets of leather with overlapping metal pieces were worn for protection. Various shaped shields, some being made of wicker (gerrhe), were carried along with the principal weapons of the period, spears, axes, swords and javelins. The personal guard of the Persian Kings were the 'Immortal' spearmen. Being the elite they wore the Persian style long skirted, loose-fitting tunics with the long flowing sleeves, over a close-fitting tunic. The overgarment was hitched up in front and secured with a fringed waist sash; it was colourfully decorated overall. The hair and beard were arranged in the Persian fashion, around the head was a wide twisted cord fillet. This elite corps carried a spear and bows and arrows. In battle many Persian soldiers wore a loose cloth which framed the face concealing the lower jaw. The higher the crown of this headgear the higher the rank of the person.

As most Greek plays are concerned with war, soldiers and their implements of war are very prominent. Bronze seemed to have been the metal used for their weapons and armour. The Greek *hoplite* or heavily armoured citizen infantry, was the most formidable soldier of the period. Their harsh

Assyrian

Assyrian

Assyrian

Assyrian

Assyrian helmets and weapons

62

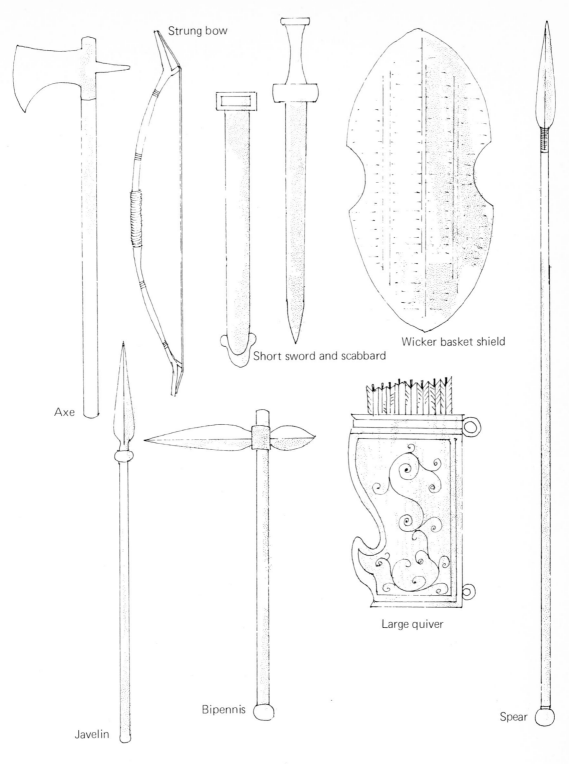

Strung bow

Short sword and scabbard

Wicker basket shield

Axe

Javelin

Bipennis

Large quiver

Spear

Persian weapons

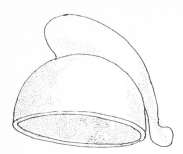

Persian bronze

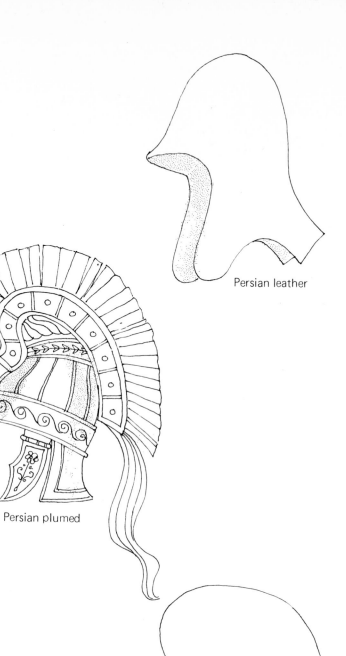

Persian leather

Persian plumed

Persian

Persian leather

Persian helmets

64

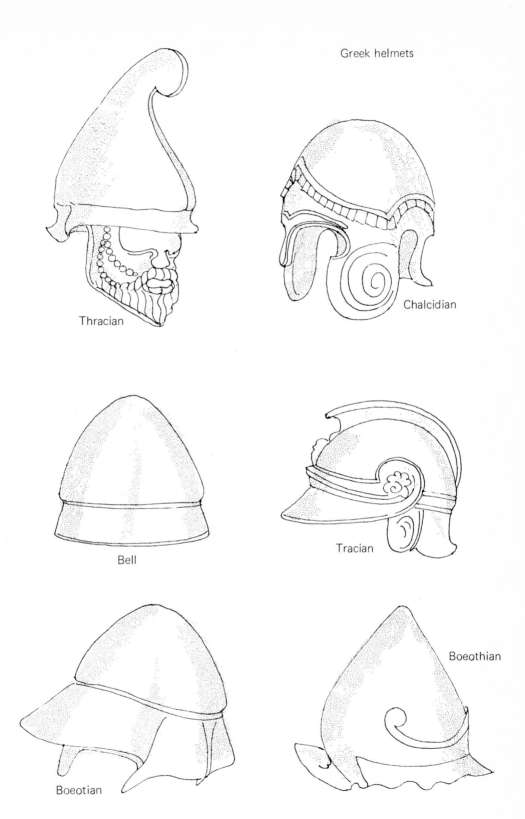

Greek helmets

Thracian

Chalcidian

Bell

Tracian

Boeotian

Boeothian

65

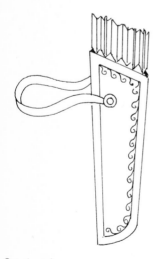

Greek bow

Greek quiver

discipline and fanatical refusal to yield ground made them ideal soldiers. Over their simple basic chiton which reached down to about middle thigh length was a composite flexible leather-backed corselet which was covered with small overlapping metal plates. Over this body-covering were two shoulder pieces which were tied at the back, then pulled over the shoulders and laced at the front. The lower half of the body was protected, as were sometimes the shoulders by strips of leather known as *pteruges* (feathers) usually weighted with small metal plates.

For earlier Greek plays the 'bell' *cuirass* must be worn. This was a two piece, waist length armour covering made from bronze. It consisted of a front and back plate which was secured at the shoulders and sides by hinges. About the middle of the sixth century this bell shape armour was abandoned and the previously described linen or leather-backed cuirass became popular and cheaper to make. The 'muscled' cuirass usually for officers remained until the end of the Roman era. The legs were protected by bronze greaves which were worn between the skin and the ankle. They fitted closely round the lower leg following the contours of the anatomy of the leg that sometimes no extra fastening was required, otherwise rings and straps were fitted. Sandals of open-work leather lacing were worn but many vase paintings from which much of the information is taken, show that the feet were more often than not bare.

As was the custom, all hoplites were committed in finding their own expensive equipment; only the wealthier citizens could afford to purchase and keep in good order so many of the items required, there was therefore a variety of styles worn. The helmet was no exception, there were several types of Greek helmet, evolving from the Doric, Ionic and Corinthian Orders. There were others which are also illustrated in this book. The Doric-style helmet, completely covered the face except for two small openings for the eyes. Fixed at the top of the helmet was usually a large horsehair crest, this was more than an ornament, it gave extra protection from sword strokes. This type of helmet is unsuitable for theatrical purposes, unless it is a non-speaking part; being closed in, it would curtail good voice delivery and hide all facial expression. The Ionic-style helmet was made with two easy moveable hinged cheek flaps, ideal for all stage purposes. Most helmets were fitted with crests and indeed were an essential feature of Greek helmets. Later helmets

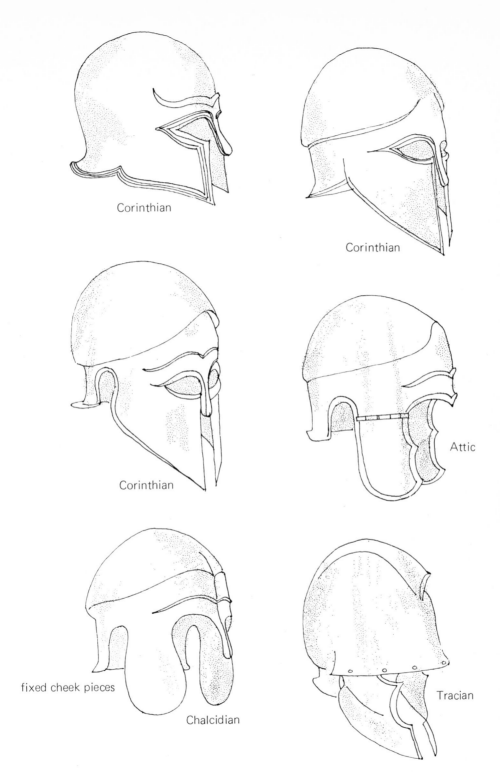

Corinthian

Corinthian

Corinthian

Attic

fixed cheek pieces

Chalcidian

Tracian

Greek helmets

67

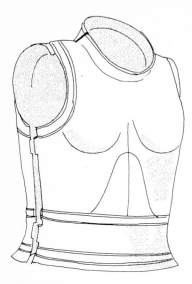

'Bell' cuirass worn by the early Greek warriors

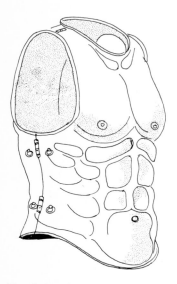

Muscled cuirass worn by both Greek and Roman warriors

were worn without crests. The Corinthian type helmet, was made in one piece with fixed nose and cheek pieces. All helmets were lined with felt, leather or thick linen.

A short thrusting *sword* was carried hanging from a strap over the right shoulder, they were about 60 cm (24 in.) long with a leaf-shaped blade. The chief weapon of the hoplite was the *spear*, it was long, some 2 to 3 m (6ft 6in. to 9 ft 9 in.) often pointed at both ends with leaf-shaped spear head and butt ends. Peculiar to the hoplites was the massive round shield measuring 1 m (39 in.) or more in diameter; which was called an *aspis*, made from seven or more layers of tough ox hide. The outer layer having bosses of metal in various shapes; which when used in close-quarter fighting was pushed against the enemy to crush him. They were usually painted overall with designs and motifs and various emblems and blazons. It was designed so that the support arm-band and the handgrip, which was placed near the rim, positioned the shield projected to protect half of the holder and the other half of the hoplite on the bearers immedeate left; this made the famous phalanx style of formation possible to manoeuvre. Many battle shields were made from wood then covered with hide or from wicker and covered with leather; in addition some shields had a fringed leather curtain hanging down to break the impact and protect the soldiers legs from arrows, darts and sword blows; they often bore the bearer's unit insignia.

A symbol of the Spartan soldier was the scarlet cloak he wore. The Roman army was the finest military force in the then known world and the soldiers are represented in many biblical and modern plays. It was at first a citizen's army, then as it developed it was formed from every country which they conquered. The information and the formation of the Roman armour is gathered mainly from statues and columns erected over the centuries and the various discoveries from excavations and archaeological examples.

The *Roman legionaires* dress was the *helmet*, body armour, sword, spear and greaves. The earlier galea or leather helmet was replaced by the bronze helmets. The bronze helmets resembled a back-to-front 'jockey cap' with cheek-guards. Worn with this type of helmet was the Greek type *lorica hamata* and *lorica segmanta mail shirts*, as body protection. Although the latter was worn the most popular form of protection was that of the lorica segementata a well designed arrangement of six metal strips. This corselet of circular

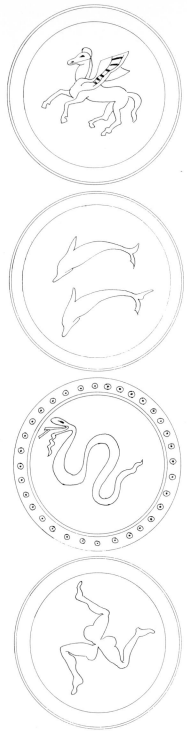

Greek Hoplite emblazoned
shields

iron bands was tied at the back and front with tag loops. The five plated shoulder pieces were attached to the two hinged half sections of the collar piece, then strapped to the girdle plates. The corselet was worn over a brown woollen tunic, this reached to just above the knee, with short, wide sleeves. The *focale* or *military scarf* which acted both as a sweat-cloth and a protection against the armour chafing the neck, was also probably of the same colour and material.

The bronze helmet was now reinforced with iron skull, neck-guard and cheek pieces. The crest was worn purely for ceremonial purposes. The legionaires *footwear* was the caliga, a heavy boot with hobnails, this boot was quite short, fastening just around the ankle. Military buskins with animal skins and decoration were worn by the officers, these were usually calf-length and made of leather.

Basically there were two types of *shield*: the scutum which was usually long, rectangular and convex, this was made of wood and covered in leather, round the edges it was bound with thin bronze or iron and reinforced in the corners with iron plates. The clipeus or round shield was often made of bronze but as this was somewhat expensive it was not so popular. The scutum measured about 1.6 m (5ft) and on the centre boss was engraved the name and unit of the bearer. The shield was either painted or decorated with metal pieces which represented some motif episemes which gave the bearer some protection from evil.

The Roman legionaires weapons varied but for many centuries they were equipped with the pugio a *dagger* of some 50 cm (18 in.) long, used by the legionary for domestic purposes. The gladius or short sword had a blade of 50 cm (18 in.) long and 5 cm (2 in.) wide, the scabbard followed the shape of the distinctive blade shape. The pilum was a heavy *javelin* with a wooden shaft of some 2.5 m (7 ft) long, so shaped as to take a small pyramid tipped 50 cm long soft-iron shaft. Each soldier carried two of these pila.

Among the *paraphenalia* that the Roman soldier had to carry on his back, a weight of some 20 kilos (25 lb), was his weapons, cooking equipment, bedding, spade, pick-axe, drinking flask (mixture of vinegar and water), and a string bag which probably contained his fortnight's ration of flour. All this was supported by a pole two metres long, forked at one end. Into this fork was tied a kit-bag which contained his sagum (cloak), and other bits and pieces of a personal nature.

Roman standard bearer with lion skin headgear

Battle axe

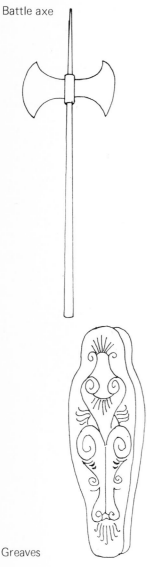

Greaves

The calf-length *breeches* were now worn by all ranks. The standard-bearer retained his unusual headwear, that of a wolf, lion, leopard or bear skin which covered his head and his face appeared between its jaws. The standard was reverenced by the legionary and when not being carried was kept in a shrine in the praetorum (headquarters).

Although mentioned here as part of the Roman soldiers' equipment the *cloaks* are essentially a part of the costume department. The legionary wore during the winter period a brick-coloured cloak, the officers had a white one, the generals were distinguished by wearing a scarlet wool cloak embroidered with gold lace. With the decline of the Roman Empire there grew up another Empire, the Byzantine Empire, whose capital city was Constantinople. Soldiers from this Eastern Empire dressed very much like the Roman warriors, consisting of half-armour, large round shield, a long sword and all the soldiers wore breeches. The helmets differed from the Roman type in that they left the face uncovered and had a deeper brim. Because there is no great literature on this period regarding the theatre there is no need to comment too deeply on their military equipment.

Included in the Romanesque period of soldiers must also be mentioned the Barbarians, Gauls, Franks, Vikings, Anglo-Saxons, Carolingians and the Normans, however briefly. Many of their uniforms and weapons were illustrated throughout the plates and marginal drawings.

The *Gauls* wore very little, a pair of trousers gathered in at the ankle, and a coarse woollen cloak attached at the shoulder with a pin or clasp. His primitive shield was a woven wicker covered with leather. A helmet (worn only by the chiefs) was of either bronze or iron. Protective clothing such as breast-plates and chain-mail existed but were little used, they followed the Greek style. The most favoured weapon was the iron sword, which was 1 m long and 5 cm wide.

The *Franks* apart from their extraordinary hair styles and large moustaches dressed in animal skins (and simple clothes) and long trousers in cross thonging. They carried shields both round and rectangular and their weapons were frames (spears), angon (javelin), francisca (throwing axe) and a scramasax (a large cutlass). The *Vikings* scorned most body-protecting armour and put great reliance on their shields, but their chiefs, wore a byrnie (a coat of mail). These byrnies were either short to the waist or reached to the knees, they were short sleeved. Helmets were worn

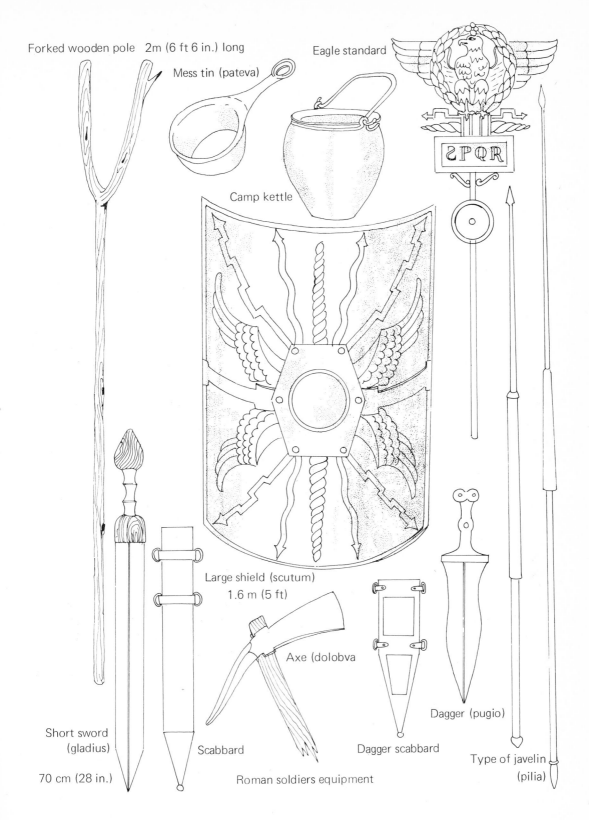

Forked wooden pole   2m (6 ft 6 in.) long

Mess tin (pateva)

Eagle standard

Camp kettle

SPQR

Large shield (scutum)
1.6 m (5 ft)

Short sword
(gladius)

70 cm (28 in.)

Scabbard

Axe (dolobva

Roman soldiers equipment

Dagger scabbard

Dagger (pugio)

Type of javelin
(pilia)

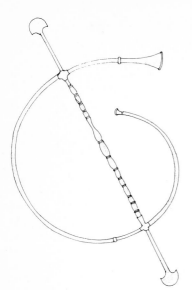

Roman Cornu

often with a figure of a boar mounted on the top, others were conical with a nose piece to guard the face, chieftains sometimes wore the horned helmet.

The *swords* were distinctive in that they tapered towards the point, but the style of hilt varied from straight to drooping. Spears of 2 m (6 ft 6 in.) long tipped with iron on one end and a leaf-shaped head on the other were used for war and hunting. The large battle axe (two-handed) was 2 m long and had a wedge shaped head. Other weapons were a throwing hammer, a small axe (bearded axe), daggers and bows and arrows. The Vikings were never content in either their uniform or their weapons and they wore mainly looted clothes and used many captured arms.

The *Anglo-Saxon warrior* was armed with a round shield, a spear and a sword or axe. The chiefs wore a short-sleeved hip length byrnie coat of mail, it was finished off at the hem line with serrations, a popular Saxon fashion design. A linen or coarse woollen tunic just above knee length was worn with full length sleeves. Under the tunic was worn trousers or hose often cross-gartered by the nobility. Helmets of both iron and leather were worn, these were in a variety of shapes, conical, round or in a phrygian style. The swords were approximately 1 m (39 in.) long, double edged with a groove running the full length of the blade. The leather scabbards were often decorated with precious stones and were attached either to a cross-belt or a waist-belt. The wooden shafted spears were over 2 m in length with a leaf shaped head. The round shields were made from wood and covered in leather reinforced with iron bands. The large two-handed axes were similar to the Viking type both in appearance and in size. Bows and arrows were used, the bow being about 1.5 m (4 ft 10in.) in length. Wooden clubs were also carried.

The *Carolingian* soldier followed the style of the earlier Roman legionary, with knee breeches and scale armour. Helmets varied from reinforced close-fitting leather to conical and brimtype shapes. Coats of mail were worn by the nobility. The round shield was the most favoured, and both the sword and the spear were the principal weapons.

The Bayeux Tapestry is the main source of information about the dress and weapons of the Normans. The hauberk (body-armour) a tunic of iron mail was made of leather covered with metal plates either sewn or rivetted on. It was short sleeved and knee length slit from the crotch down

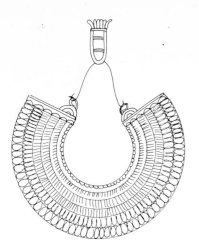

Egyptian gold neck collar

The Egyptian vulture pendant

The Egyptian vulture cobra penant

to the hem and allowed to hang down on either side. A mail hood was attached to the tunic over which was worn a conical shaped metal helmet. The helmet was made either in one piece or reinforced with iron bands in rivetted sections, with a large nasal piece. A rectangular design of lace on the upper chest closed the neck opening. Under the hauberk was a linen or woollen shorte (shirt) and braies (ankle length trousers. The offensive weapons of the Norman soldiers were the shield, sword, axe, club, bows and arrows and by the cavalry a lance with a pennant. The crossbow was used although the Bayeux Tapestry does not show it.

The *swords* were long and pointed similar to the Viking sword with a slight variation in the hilt. The sword was encased in a leather scabbard which hung from a loose waist belt. A small axe was carried in the belt. Knobbly wooden clubs and a like weapon, the mace, which had an iron head, were carried. A longbow of about 1.5 m (4 ft 10in.) was carried by the archers. The long lance was used by the cavalry with and without a pennant. The long kite-shaped shield, made from wood and covered in leather had metal bands as reinforcements was painted with various designs for recognition on the battle field. The shield was carried from a guige (strap) which went around the neck, or used to sling the shield over the back when not in use.

Although *musical instruments* come under another heading we can not leave the military section without a word about the war trumpets. Numerous types of trumpets and horns were in use from early ancient civilizations. Military trumpets were used mainly for signals and simple communication with such names as aulos, bucina, cornu, carnix and tuba, all these are illustrated.

Another important area of properties, are the costume properties, which include that of *jewellery* and other dress decoration. Again it must be emphasised that where the theatre is concerned many things step outside of the 'normal' and tend to become 'larger than life'. Jewellery comes under this category, to be seen effectively on the stage it must be made that much larger than the real thing.

The *dress accessory* which is most distinctive of the *Egyptians* and is included in all dress of the wealthier class is the collar. Worn by both men and women it was flat and round spreading from the lower neck to the shoulders and chest. The collar was made of beads joined together on a

Egyptian scarab ring

Greek/Roman earing

Greek earing

Greek brooch

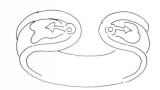

Roman bracelet

fairly flexible wire in various combinations of geometrical designs and colours, they were made from baked clay and then glazed (faience), semi-precious stones, shells and gold. Gold and enamelled metal bracelets and arm-bands of beautiful lotus or papyrus blossoms were worn along with earrings and pectorals. The pectoral was a flat large cut out design which was attached to a gold chain and hung over the collar down to just below mid-chest. The earrings were usually large discs of about 8 cm. Another favoured accessory of the Egyptians was the ornamental girdle of embroidered linen or of painted leather. The Pharaoh carried long staffs or sceptres symbols of sovereignty and dominion, the priests also carried staffs ornamented with heads of birds such as the hawk and other insignia. Fans and fly-whisks were carried and manipulated by slaves.

The *Babylonian* and the *Assyrian decoration* merged together encompassing also that of the smaller surrounding countries which included the Hebrews, Phoenicians and most of the biblical lands. Both sexes seemed to wear heavy barbaric gold bracelets, arm-bands, earrings, close-fitting 'dog collars' and circlets. Some of the statues show the male Assyrian carrying a small vessel or basket with a handle, which could have been used for carrying small personal things. The parasol or umbrella was very popular and like the fan was operated by the slaves. Unlike the other tribes the Hebrew men did not wear jewellery, but the women wore it in great profusion, including a nose ring.

Persian jewellery was similar to the Assyrian but less barbaric in appearance. Crowns, necklets, earrings and girdles were popular. Men carried walking sticks. The Greeks favoured fairly large but delicate ornamentation but more sparingly than the Assyrians. Popular among the women were the long pins or stilettos for the hair, pins with ornamental heads, fibulae in various forms, bracelets, rings with seals, earrings, pendants, brooches and necklets many of these in gold of intricate designs. Cameos and intaglios were also worn. Fans and parasols were carried by women and also by their slaves. Greek men scorned the parasol and affected long walking sticks.

The *Romans* followed the Greek styles of jewellery, sparingly at first, later being worn in greater profusion. Large earrings, bracelets, circlets all in gold were very popular among the women. Garlands of gold leaves as military awards were much sought after. In earlier times in Rome

Roman bronze bracelet arm purse

Roman necklace

Saxon ring

Saxon ring

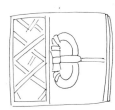

Saxon buckle

iron rings were worn. Fibulae were now in the form of brooches. The fasces (rods bound round an axe), was an insignia carried before a magistrate or a consul by a lictor denoting their official status. An ivory sceptre was borne by a consul as his symbol of office. The gold jewellery of earlier times was replaced by precious stones and enamelled inlays with brighter colours.

The *Byzantine* people wore the Egyptian style jewelled deep collar. Favoured by both men and women were earrings, brooches, bracelets, cloak-fasteners rings, pectoral crosses and belt decoration. Crowns were worn by the upper class and were inlaid with precious stones and pearls. Large hankerchiefs (mappa) were carried by the wealthier people and consuls carried a sceptre with the Imperial eagle afixed; the Emperor carried an orb and sceptre.

The *Romanesque* period developed from teutonic style of brooches (fibulae), twisted style neck and arm decoration, Celtic buckle plates, the large saucer-brooches to a more refined workmanship type of jewellery. The items were large made from precious metal and often set with rough uncut gems, and pearls.

Norman times favoured finger rings, brooches, crowns, coronets, circlets, girdles, belt-buckles. Towards the end of the twelfth century pouches or purses both large and small were worn attached to a waist belt. Sheathed daggers also hung from the waist girdle. Gloves made their appearance made from leather or fur and bejewelled and embroidered, worn only by the nobility. Plain leather or woollen mittens were worn by the lower classes.

Further emphasis must be laid down that visits to museums are most essential for further study on dress decoration. Most local museums have splendid displays of personal jewellery worn by our ancient ancestors.

Now the property master must turn to another aspect of the stage and to work along side of the set designer and or the director. Properties, furnishing and dressings of the actual scene or scenes, are stated.

Egyptian furniture was constructed on simple lines but with a wealth of detail, being made from wood, metal or ivory. The large throne type chair was often carved from wood, gold-plated and inlaid with multicoloured glass-paste, glazed terracotta and semi-precious stones. Some of the carvings were covered in silver leaf. The armrests were in the

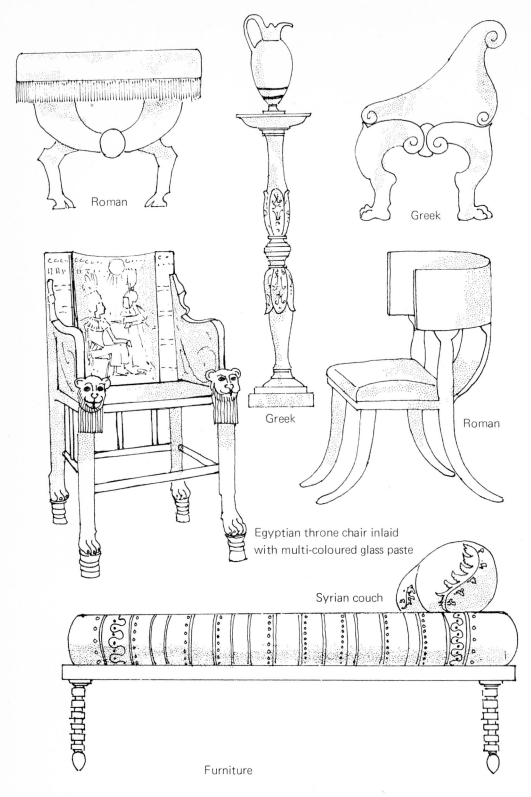

Roman

Greek

Greek

Roman

Egyptian throne chair inlaid
with multi-coloured glass paste

Syrian couch

Furniture

Egyptian flask

Egyptian flask

form of a winged serpent with the double crown. The seat of cane was supported by carved animal feet and decorated with animal heads. Other chairs and stools had rush or interwoven leather cross-tied seats. Chests and coffers were very popular, many made of stuccoed and painted wood, the panels depicted among others battle and hunting scenes; inlaid often in ivory and ebony. Beds and couches were narrow with wooden frames, short carved feline legs, mattresses were often of plaited straw. They were made with a single end-board, not at the head but at the foot, wooden head-rests were used instead of pillows, they were covered with animal skins or richly decorated overlays. Some of these beds were collapsible similar to a modern camp-bed.

Biblical style furniture covering the Babylonian and Assyrian periods included highly decorated armchairs and couches inlaid with ivory in detailed decorative designs. The chairs and couches were covered with coverlets and cushions. Furniture was made from reed, cedar, cypress or olive woods, inlaid with gold or ivory. Carpets were rich in design as were the hanging curtains and tapestries with Assyrian or Persian designs.

Greek furniture followed very closely the style and fashion of the Egyptian, but made from bronze or wood. Tripods, often of marble, with stationary legs, some of metal with detachable legs, made to unfasten from the basin and made to fold up with hinges, were very popular for both religious and domestic purposes. Thrones and foot stools, smaller chairs without arms, with legs often made of elephants' tusks; and stools without arms or backs, with carved legs of an animal design and made to fold up were the usual styles. Candelabra and lamps were supported on a base or were suspended from a chain. Tables were low not unlike a modern coffee table. Beds and couches were made with both foot and head boards, equipped with mattresses and cushions and covered with skins or drapery. In decoration and furniture the Romans, like the Greeks whom they imitated, showed great luxury and sumptuousness. The ornamentation of the triclinia or couches were wrought in ivory or silver. The candelabras were often in marble or bronze, richly chased and inlaid with silver.

Domestic and religious utensils abound throughout these periods and many good specimens are to be found in the museums.

Greek interior

The *Egyptians* used pottery often of classical design, tall shouldered, with small handles and a pointed base. Vases and jars were also made from bronze and alabaster; in various shapes and sizes, in bowl-like form with handles and others with very long necks with rings of floral decoration inlaid with coloured paste. Oil lamps with handles were also made from clay and bronze. Funerary jars with canopies of animal or human heads carved and detailed were made from alabaster granite or marble. Assorted shaped baskets were used for carrying bread, fruit, fish and other foods these being made from wicker, reeds or palm fibre. Ornate hand mirrors of highly polished copper or bronze the handles often inlaid with semi-precious stones were in popular usage.

Brace

Profiled cut-out ground row

Brace

Candelabrum cut out

Cut-out vase

Table with profiled cut-out front piece

Roman interior

Egyptian *musical instruments* were the harp, crotales and sistrums.

Most utensils changed little throughout the centuries the Biblical period followed the Egyptian style.

Although the *Greek domestic utensils* were made from pottery the graceful lines and pictorial designed fictile vases, each with their own special usage, are too numerous to

Fictile vase

Amphorae

Drinking horn

Vase

Greek vase

Fictile vase

Pateras

Lamp

Grecian vases

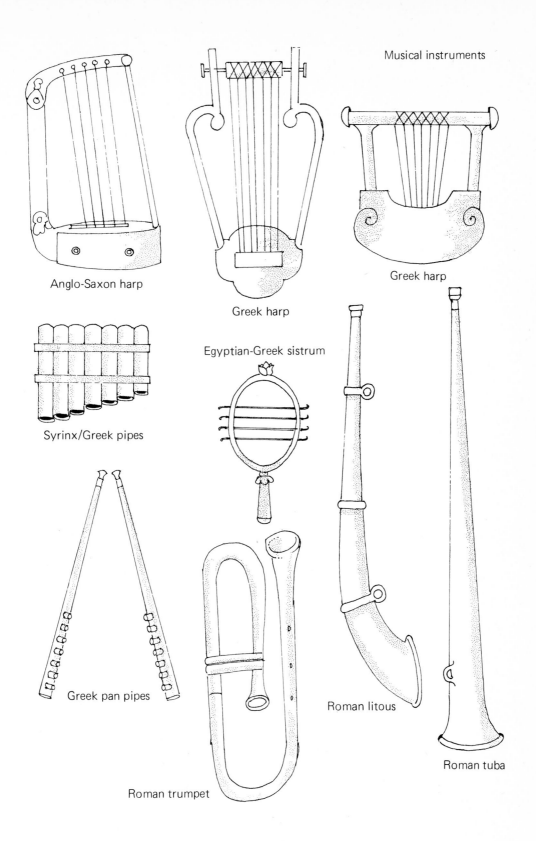

Anglo-Saxon harp

Greek harp

Greek harp

Musical instruments

Syrinx/Greek pipes

Egyptian-Greek sistrum

Greek pan pipes

Roman trumpet

Roman litous

Roman tuba

81

Norman jugs

Roman vase (Britain)

Norman plate

Roman vase (Britain)

Roman vase (Britain

Roman flask (Britain)

Roman vase (Britain(

Roman/Norman vases

mention, as many as possible of these amphorae have been illustrated. Rhytons or drinking horns were carved with a handle and finished with an animal head at the base. Fruit and food wicker baskets were in use, also deeper baskets were used as work baskets. Kylix (wine cups) and oil jars were made from pottery.

Torches of bronze were carried or hung on the walls. Folding tripods were made from metal with straight or carved legs in various designs.

Musical instruments were very popular with the Greeks. The lyre and the double flute (which was played to accompany dancing) were part of a wealthy boy's education. The lyre was the most commonly played and was made in a variety of shapes as illustrated. There was also the cithara, syrinx (pan-pipes) and harps.

Roman utensils were as in the previous centuries made from pottery in both the glazed and unglazed variety.

The *Byzantine* period used very much the same.

The *Romanesque* era brought a lower standard in the making of utensils compared with the classical lines of the Greek and Roman, but utensils in glass, iron and bronze reached a more advanced stage. The metalwork included the manufacture of cups, spoons and plates in tin pewter and gold.

Papier mâché and *papier mâché* pulp are ideal for many of the properties mentioned, the process is simple and very cheap, there are however other techniques. Glass fibre, polyester resins and cold cast metals are just a few of the new materials to make many of the 'props' that much easier. Through the medium of these techniques the reproduction of armour and weapons makes the play that much more realistic.

Saxon wooden bucket

Viking drinking horn

Saxon drinking horn

SCENIC DESIGN

At the outset a design is a 'picture' of the proposed stage set and will have the same problems of composition as any other picture; therefore all the elements must be correctly balanced to produce a pleasing and practical visual scene, which must be the designers primary consideration. Therefore the media to achieve this must be studied and the materials and techniques of the theatre applied intelligently.

Architectual forms provide an answer to the habits, customs, thoughts and hopes of the people without which the historical events of the epoch would lose their significance.

The basic architecture and general appearance of the period must be incorporated into the stage design to reproduce the correct atmosphere.

An analysis of the typical architecture of the periods must involve the planning and arranging of buildings, their construction and treatment, character, form and development. Pillars and columns, in which these periods abound, have a large part in the construction of buildings so their position in relationship within and without a building, their structure and ornamentation, must be taken into account.

In the Egyptian era religion and architecture were interwoven as shown by the giant pyramids and tombs erected for the preservation of the body. Dwelling houses were looked upon as temporary abodes and the tombs as a permanent dwelling place.

Egyptian architecture is distinguished by its gigantic scale, the massive walls and pillars with their carved and painted capitals with symbolic floral motifs, these were highly decorative and brightly coloured. Tall obelisks in pairs were erected at the entrances to the temples standing at least 22 m high and 3 m square at the base. The interiors of the temples and palaces were highly decorated with pictures, alongside the hieroglyphic system, graphically record-

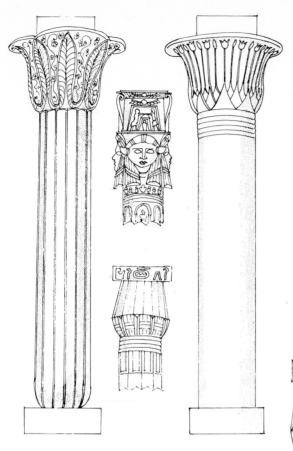

Egyptian pillars and capitals

Egyptian set piece

ing events of social history. Paintings, more than mouldings, were characteristic of the symbolic decoration which were carried out mainly in blue, red and yellow. These motifs of a symbolic nature often appeared on the costume and furniture.

The monumental style architecture included sphinxes which were mythical creatures with lion bodies and human and animal heads. The general character of Egyptian architecture was the horizontal with square shaped openings.

In *Babylionian* and *Assyrian architecture* the pillar played a lesser role in the construction, brick built towers being more favoured. The whole effect of their palaces and temples was towering buildings on large platforms with broad stairways and ramps. Flanking the portals of the palaces were colossal figures of winged bulls and large bas-reliefs.

Semi-circular arches were employed both inside and out in Assyrian architecture. Distinctive of the Assyrian style, at the later period they incorporated in the construction tall painted columns with highly carved capitals in the form of human and animal heads and plants. Walls were decorated with glazed brick pictures of mythological forms.

The *Persians* took over many of the influences of architecture from Assyrian and Egyptian styles, such as the sculptured animals, the bas-reliefs and the glazed colourful brickwork, but they were far superior to the Egyptian in their decoration.

Greek style architecture had a low and horizontal form, temples usually being only one storey high, with no outer walls, the flat roof being supported by columns which played an important part in Greek construction of buildings.

The Greek columns came in orders, the most robust and dignified was that of the Doric order, the Parthenon being one of the best examples. Next was the refined slender Ionic order which had scrolls on two sides only of its distinctive capital. The Corinthian order although little used by the Greeks, had an elaborate acanthus capital. Two lesser types were the draped female sculptured figures of the canephora and the caryatid.

Greek architecture had a flowing delicate simplicity of moulding which enhanced the line of the buildings. Acanthus leaf and scroll work were an important part of Greek ornamentation. Many of the sculptured reliefs and friezes can be seen with many of the sculptured figures in a number of museums.

Persian set pieces

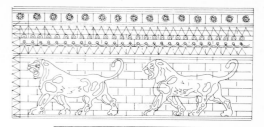

Centre set piece ground row

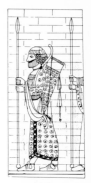

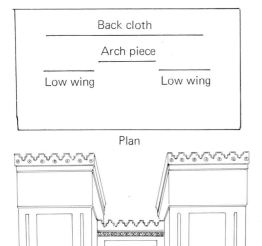

Back cloth

Arch piece

Low wing   Low wing

Plan

Wing   Wing

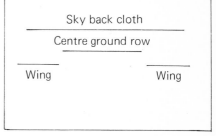

Sky back cloth

Centre ground row

Wing   Wing

Plan

Arch piece   Low wing piece   Assyrian set pieces

Canephora

Sanctuary

Caryatid

Drapes or painted cyclorama

Sanctuary set piece

Canephora
wing piece

Caryatid
wing piece

Plan

Greek set

Dwelling houses were built windowless in the front, being lit from the inner courtyard which was open, with the rooms spaced around it. Doorways and openings were square-headed and crowned with a cornice. Wall paintings (murals) and mosaics were the popular form of the interiors. Colonades were a freature of Greek architecture.

The *Romans* revolutionised wall construction by inventing and using cement. Notwithstanding they adopted the column and beam construction of the Greeks. They continued the Orders of the Greek columns. The Tuscan and Composite were added, the Tuscan was a plain version of the Doric whilst the Composite was a combination of the Ionic and Corinthian capitals, giving an ornate appearance. The Romans often superimposed the orders one with the other during their building. The Roman Ionic order was less refined than the Greek. The keynote of the Roman architecture was the impression of vastness and magnificence.

Fresco paintings, coloured marbles and mosaics were used for interior decoration depicting mythological and historical decor. The acanthus scroll was specially characteristic of Roman ornamentation and on friezes. Colour was used in great contrasts of light and shade, reds, blacks, blues. Floors were laid in mosaics of geometrical designs.

Roman doors and openings were both square after the Greek style and semi-circular headed, this being an important decorative feature.

Byzantine architecture followed the domical method of construction. The walls of brick were internally finished in a rich lavishly coloured marble. Openings were spanned with semi-circular arches. Columns played a subordinate feature, used as interior supports rather than superstructure support.

Elaborate mosaic art was the scheme of ornamentation of the Byzantine period.

Romanesque architecture followed the influence of the Roman craftsmanship in the construction of the walls but of a much lower standard, being very roughly built. Buttresses became a feature along with attached columns with rough capitals, which supported semi-circular arches making wall arching as a decorative feature. Columns were either cylindrical of a stubby proportion or made as massive piers, in a variation of Ionic or Corinthian capitals. Low rounded arches were prevalent. Ornamentation was frequently roughly carved grotesque figurework. Interior mosaics were replaced by frescoes. Castle interiors were of stone with wall decorated hangings or murals. The impressive or Romanesque architecture was of a cold fortress-like greyness lacking in both charm and beauty. The earlier open fire in the centre of the main hall was replaced by a purpose-built chimney in the wall.

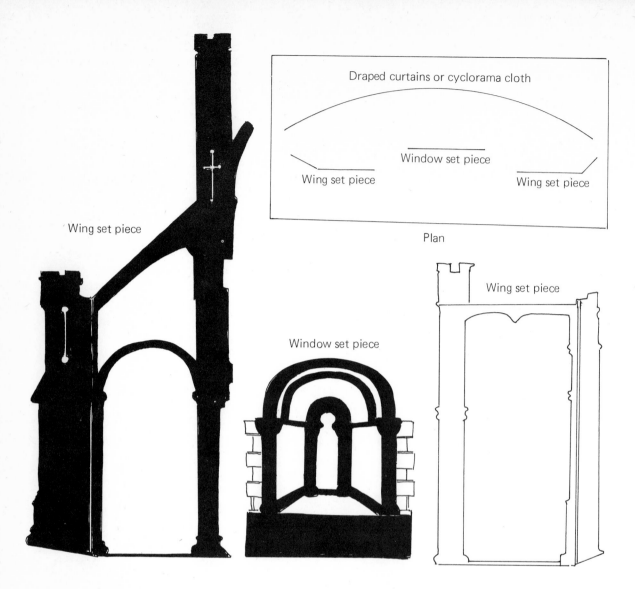

Draped curtains or cyclorama cloth

Window set piece

Wing set piece

Wing set piece

Plan

Wing set piece

Window set piece

Wing set piece

An impressionistic historical set

The foregoing is merely a very brief analysis of architecture spanning many hundreds of years it is impossible to go into greater detail other than to put the would-be designer on the right track.

Study the period of the chosen play carefully, researching everything possible that is in the slightest way connected with that particular moment in history. Simplicity of a setting does not imply an amateurish outlook, as a matter of fact a simple design may surpass the large structual complex sets in artistic results. Remember too that the use of drapes (curtains) creates great possibilities.

Research however does involve a great deal of work in museums, public libraries, art galleries in fact anywhere

where there is an historical concatenation. The dramatic qualities of scenery (the scenic pieces) are of course, achieved through the designers ability to deal with the variety of subjects and to use them in a visual art form. The main quality is remembering that the theatre is 'larger than life' and to use proportion in this sense, yet to still seem architectually logical.

The environment of an historical-dominated play is usually real, the scenic-designers problem is to create, with the first impression, through a selection of realistic details and shapes, the mood and its relationship to the action and characters. To show a specific time in the historical past that will prepare a state of mind in the audience.

Norman period set

Norman window piece

Pillory

Rough wood seats

Stocks

STAGE LIGHTING

The history of stage lighting over the centuries of theatre-craft has seen many changes. From the dependence of daylight, flaming torches, and blazing pineknots in iron cressets to the flickering candles of the seventeenth and the gas jets of the nineteenth centuries, and the sophisticated art of stage lighting today.

Today stage settings are dependent on illumination, therefore stage lighting plays an important part in the final presentation of historical plays. The obvious reason for illumination on the stage is visibility, to ascertain that the audience is able to observe all the happenings that they are supposed to see, or the reverse, not to see. Light on the stage should be used to express reality (or unreality). Obvious light sources, eg. light through a window, or open doorway, should be apparent. The audience must feel that the light they see, source and direction, is within the realms of possibility. Lighting should be used to bring all the visual aspects of the stage together. It should not be used to just illuminate the actors, actresses, scenic effects, properties and costume; but like a painter's brush to give light and shade, brilliance and shadows on certain parts of the general decor. Special costumes may need accentuating, but everything must be balanced by illumination to convey mood and feeling to the audience.

Colour is dependent on light, but colour added to the final composition makes the dramatic effect even greater.

Coloured light has a distinct advantage over painted pigment colours, they can change in quality and intensity following the everchanging mood of the historical drama.

Light and colour symbolize and help to create the asmosphere of the play and I hope the historical costume and set designers will familiarise themselves with this very important and absorbing feature which plays such a part in the success — or failure — of any production.

CHOOSING A PLAY

Aeschylus (525-456 BC)
The Suppliant Women
The Persians
Seven against Thebes
Prometheus Bound
The Oresteia (Trilogy)

Aristophanes (448-385 BC)
The Acharnians
The Knights
The Clouds
The Wasps
Peace
The Birds
Lysistrata
Thesmophoriazusae
Ecclesiazusae

Euripides (484-406 BC)
Alcestis
Medea
Hippolytus
Iphigenia in Tauris
Helen
Hecuba
Iphigenia in Aulis
The Bacchae
Cyclops

Sophocles (496-406 BC)
Ajax
Antigone
Electra
Oedipus at Colonus

Oedipus Rex
Philoctetes
The Women of Trachis

The stage is a fascinating world where the past comes back to the present to live again, where actors and technicians work side by side to create, from the imaginary world of the writers, a harmony of assorted effects and efforts. The main problem in producing a play is to find the correct vehicle. So many different factors must influence the selection of a play, and the choice must be governed by a series of sound reasons, eg the suitability of staging and the number of people involved. Many plays have certain and obvious drawbacks for the small companies, schools and amateur dramatics.

For any group embarking on a theatrical venture, catalogues of plays from a good bookshop can at this stage prove indispensable. These catalogues give a brief run-down of plays and stage-settings and the number of people required for the cast. The main objective is to aim as high as possible; Aristophanes, Euripides, Shakespeare, Shaw — if you start at the top you have the very best dramatists working for you.

As a guide to the periods in this volume I have compiled a list of plays which, over a period of years, have been performed and presented by many theatre groups, dramatic societies and schools. Remarkably the majority of these plays can, with a little forethought and intelligent application, be staged with the utmost simplicity. My obvious first choices are from the surviving plays of the Greek dramatists, Aeschylus, Aristophanes, Euripides, Menander, Sophocles and from the Roman dramatists Terence and Seneca.

All plays, both ancient and modern, of the Homeric tales and

Menander (342-292 BC)
Hero
Woman from Samos
Epitrepontes
Rape of the Locks

Greek Mythology can be included.

From Shakespeare's pen the Greek play *Troilus and Cressida* is recommended.

The Egyptian period as well as that of the Hebrew and Assyrians are well covered by the religious plays of the Old Testament.

For the Roman period there are

Terence (195-159 BC)	Seneca (c 4 BC - AD 65)
Andria	*Hercules Furens*
Hecyra	*Phaedra*

William Shakespeare *Antony and Cleopatra*
George Bernard Shaw *Caesar and Cleopatra, Androcles and the Lion*
Robert Sherwood *The Road to Rome*
F.M.A. de Voltaire *Brutus*
John Masefield *The Tragedy of Pompey the Great, Good Friday*
Charles Rann Kennedy *The Terrible Meek*
Lew Wallace *Ben Hur*

For the late Byzantine and Romanesque periods, Shakespeare's plays
A Winter's Tale, King Lear, Macbeth

Maurice Maeterlinck
Pelléas and Mélisande, The Death of Tintagiles

All Arthurian and Irish folk plays and Wagnerian operas are based on the costumes and settings of this period.

INDEX

Anglo-Saxon 50, 70, 72
Animal skin 10, 69, 70, 77
Architecture 7, 84, 86, 89, 90
Armour 8, 40, 41, 58, 61, 66, 68, 70, 72, 83
Assyrian 10, 17, 20, 21, 24, 25, 61, 74, 77, 86
Athenian 28

Babylonian 10, 17, 21, 24, 28, 43, 47, 50, 61
Barbaric 47, 50
Beard 14, 19, 24, 28, 43, 47, 50, 61
Belt 13, 14, 17, 19, 20, 32, 39, 41, 50, 51, 72, 75
Bishop 57
Bliaut 50, 51
Boots 19, 41, 45, 57, 69
Boys 36, 43
Breeches 41, 45, 47, 50, 70, 72
Buskins 41, 69
Byzantine 7, 10, 39, 45, 47, 50, 57, 70, 75, 83, 89

Cap 25, 27, 28, 51, 57
Cape 14, 45, 47
Carolingian 70, 72
Celtic 47
Chain mail 19, 61, 70
Chemise 51
Children 16, 27, 36
Chiton 28, 32, 36, 38, 43, 66
Chlamys 28, 36
Clerics 51
Cloak 40, 45, 47, 50, 51, 69, 70
Coat 20, 61

Collar 14, 16, 20, 24, 57, 58, 69, 73, 74, 75
Costume 6, 7, 8, 9, 11, 17, 20, 58, 73, 86, 92
Crown 16, 75
Cuirass 32, 41, 66

Dye 7, 9, 10, 13, 14, 24, 36, 43

Egyptian 6, 7, 8, 10, 11, 14, 17, 20, 24, 58, 61, 73, 74, 77, 78, 79, 84, 86

Fibula 28, 32, 36, 40, 50, 51, 74, 75
Footwear 14, 16, 19, 24, 41, 45, 50, 69
Franks 70
Furniture 7, 8, 75, 86

Gauls 70
Girdle 13, 14, 20, 27, 28, 32, 43, 47, 51, 57, 69, 74, 75
Girls 36, 43
Greaves 32, 41, 66
Greek 6, 10, 20, 28, 36, 38, 40, 41, 43, 45, 61, 66, 70, 74, 77, 79, 83, 86, 89

Habit
Hair 14, 16, 19, 20, 24, 27, 28, 36, 43, 45, 47, 50, 51, 61
Hat 16, 19, 47
Headband 19, 20
Headdress 14, 16, 20, 25, 28
Hebrew 24, 25, 26, 27
Helmet 8, 9, 32, 41, 43, 47, 58, 61, 66, 68, 69, 70, 72, 73
Himaton 28, 32, 40, 43
Hood 20, 40, 45, 47, 50, 51, 73

Hoplites 61, 66, 68

Jacket 41
Jewellery 7, 8, 16, 19, 24, 27, 36, 51, 73, 74, 75

Legionaire 47, 68, 69
Loin cloth 6, 7, 13, 36, 58

Make-Up 16
Mede 24
Men 11, 13, 16, 17, 19, 20, 24, 28, 36, 43, 45, 47, 50, 73, 74
Mercenaries 61
Mitre 27, 57
Monk 51
Moustache 19, 28, 47, 50, 61
Musical instruments 73, 79, 83

Norman 50, 70, 72, 73, 75

Ornamentation 7, 16, 27, 51, 66, 74, 77, 89

Persian 10, 17, 20, 24, 25, 61, 74, 77, 86
Phoenicians 74
Phyrgian 32, 47, 51, 72
Priest 25

Roman 6, 10, 36, 41, 43, 45, 47, 50, 57, 68, 69, 70, 72, 74, 77, 83, 89
Romanesque 7, 8, 10, 45, 70, 75, 83, 89

Sandals 10, 14, 16, 19, 27, 36, 51, 57, 66

Shawl, 14, 17, 19, 20, 24
Shoes 24
Shorts 41
Skirt 13, 14, 32, 50, 51
Soldiers 8, 17, 19, 21, 24, 28, 32, 41, 45, 47, 58, 61, 66, 68, 69, 70, 73
Spartans 28, 32, 68
Stage lighting 8, 9, 58, 92
Stage properties 6, 8, 17, 32, 58, 73, 75, 92
Stage settings 6, 7, 8, 58, 84, 90, 92
Standard bearer 43, 70
Stockings 50
Sun hat (Petasos) 28, 36, 45, 47

Teutonic 47, 50
Toga 10, 36, 38, 43, 45
Trousers 72, 73
Tunic 13, 14, 17, 19, 20, 24, 25, 27, 45, 47, 50, 51, 57, 58, 61, 69, 72, 73
Tunica 36, 38, 39, 41, 43, 45
Turban 19, 25, 27, 47

Utensils 8, 77, 79, 83

Veil 45, 47
Vikings 70, 72

Weapons 8, 17, 24, 32, 41, 61, 68, 70, 72, 73, 83
Wigs 14, 16, 17, 36, 58
Women 7, 10, 11, 14, 16, 19, 24, 27, 28, 32, 36, 43, 45, 47, 50, 51, 73, 74